Lloyd John Ogilvie

LIFE
AS IT
WAS
MEANT
TO BE

Regal
Books

A Division of G/L Publications
Ventura, California, U.S.A.

The foreign language publishing of all Regal books is under the direction of GLINT. GLINT provides financial and technical help for the adaptation, translation and publishing of books in more than 85 languages for millions of people worldwide.

For more information write: GLINT, P.O. Box 6688, Ventura, California 93006

Published by Regal Books
A Division of G/L Publications
Ventura, California 93006
Printed in U.S.A.

Library of Congress Catalog Card No. 80-50541
ISBN: 0-8307-0740-9
Code Number: 51 087 05

Contents

Introduction

This is a book about life. Life as it was meant to be. *Authentic Life.*

In a world of replicas, facsimiles and cheap distortions, we long for the authentic. The word defines the dimensions of our quest. Authentic means of "undisputable origin, original, consistent with the facts, congruent with reality, trustworthy and true." That's exactly what we all want when it comes to living this many splendored thing we call life.

I have often wondered what it must have been like to hear the proclamation of the gospel of life in the first century—before the profoundly simple message of life in Christ and His life in us was veneered with highly polished theology and efforts to make it philosophically respectable. That sent me back to the essential preaching and writing of the apostle Paul, a man in Christ, whose basic message was, "For to me, to live is Christ" (Phil. 1:21). In my review of the dates of writing of the books of the New Testament, I found that the apostle's letters to the Thessalonians were written in the year

A.D. 50, about 15 years after his conversion and less than 20 years after the crucifixion of Jesus. The more I reread these Epistles, the more I felt I was in touch with "pure Paul" before his writing style was perfected. The early date of their writing made them all the more attractive and vital. The unstudied, personal impact of the letters read less like a treatise and more like a personal friend's urgent response to authentic spiritual need in living life as it was meant to be.

A careful study of the context of 1 and 2 Thessalonians, coupled with a review of Acts 17, draws back the veil of time for us to watch the drama of primitive Christianity in action. Paul wrote these friendship letters out of deep love for the Thessalonians and in response to specific problems they were facing in living the adventuresome life in Christ he had taught them during his brief stay in the strategic city of northern Greece. These struggles of the new Christians are not unlike those we face today. What Paul wrote them to sustain them is an excellent charter for our quest for authentic Christianity.

My study of the Thessalonian letters led me to a prolonged visit in Salonika, also called Thessaloniki, the teeming harbor city in northern Greece. This is the site of ancient Thessalonica of Macedonia where Paul, Silas and Timothy ministered and established a strong church. My stay there was a part of a retracing of the travels of Paul's missionary journeys. It was exciting to arrive in Kavala, the site of ancient Neapolis, and drive through the cut in the mountains to the ruins of Philippi. Then I followed Paul's route through the mountains west to Thessalonica, Paul's second stop in his Macedonian ministry. I'll never forget the excitement I felt when I drove through the city, relishing the opportunity to linger there to study in depth the apostle Paul's first letters. Each day I would take the Greek text of the New Testament and sit on the wharf of the harbor or wander through the streets. Then late in the afternoon and into the night, I wrote insights which are the substance of this book.

Ancient Thessalonica was a crucial place for Paul to preach the gospel and establish a vital church. The city has had one of the world's great dockyards throughout history. It has remained one of the strategic trade and industrial cities of the world. The original name of the city was Thermai, because of the Thermaic Gulf on which it stands. In B.C. 315 Cassander rebuilt the city and renamed it Thessalonica, the name of his wife, daughter of Philip of Macedon and half-sister of Alexander the Great. Thessalonica was distinguished not only for its port but because the Roman road, the Via Egnatia, was the main street of the city. It was the link between Rome and the East. No wonder the city was nicknamed "the lap of the Roman Empire."

After Philippi, Thessalonica was Paul's second stop in his Macedonian ministry. The church he founded there was one of the most dynamic of all he established. What happened to people in Thessalonica was bound to spread to the then known world. The Roman road and the influence of seamen and traders carried the gospel to the far reaches of civilization. If the gospel could work in Thessalonica, a tough seaport, it could work anywhere! We can understand why the survival of the church there was so important to the apostle Paul.

Spending a period of time in Thessalonica gave me a feel for the people unique to northern Greece and southern Europe. They are a special breed—tough-minded, strong-willed, highly emotional. One morning as I studied on the wharf I saw a group of weather-beaten and intense stevedores engaged in a heated, emotional confrontation over an insignificant issue. I talked with people of all classes and types in this modern seaport, and it gave me a sense of the unpolished, straightforward people who are not unlike those to whom Paul ministered. The city still has its rough-hewn fishermen, dockhands and sharp dealing businessmen, very much like the people who both responded to and resisted Paul's preaching of the gospel. But a vigilant church was born. And Paul had its welfare and problems on his heart. That's why he wrote his first Epistle to the church at Thessalonica. The new Christians were in trouble: resistance and persecution met their newfound faith in Christ and the church was disturbed by problems from within and without its infant life.

But the gospel had made a beachhead. The church would survive. The living Christ was on the move, establishing a worldwide faith for all nations. Thessalonica was strategic in His plan. The cosmopolitan city became a stronghold for world evangelization. And Paul was the Lord's relentless, adventuresome missionary.

Paul's letters to the Thessalonians deal with what it means to be a Christian in word and deed, life and death, joy and persecution; and they help us to be nothing less for our time. They reveal the true, genuine, real life which the Thessalonians experienced when they heard the gospel of Jesus Christ, and turned from idols to a liberated life of integrity and wholeness. The assurance the people needed to grow on, and the wisdom they required to face persecution and rejection, motivated a letter of true friendship from Paul, the epistle of a friend who really cared. The more I studied the Thessalonian letters inductively, the more aware I was that what Paul explained about the authentic life in Christ is the need of the church today. Thus the following expositions of the Thessalonian epistles.

This book is not intended to be a word-by-word, verse-by-verse exposition. Rather, it seeks to catch the main currents of the fast-moving river of Paul's thought and apply them to today. I did my basic study there in Thessalonica with two focuses in mind: (1) the needs of people and (2) what Paul wrote with such empathy and incisive love.

In each chapter I take a portion of each letter as the basis of my thought. I have searched for what I call the jugular vein—the key verse which unlocks the meaning. A topical expository style results. My illustrations are about real people who are struggling with the same problems as those ancient Thessalonians. What has resulted is not a critical commentary as much as a readable magna carta for growing, adventuring Christians today.

As in most of my writings, this book has had a three-year evolution. The first year I lived with the text of the Thessalonian letters in my own personal devotions. The second year, which included my visit to Thessalonica, was a scholarly penetration into the Greek text and the historical context. The third year was given over to preaching and teaching what the Lord had given to me and, subsequent to each presentation, the actual writing of these chapters. It has been a rewarding time.

When I shared the results of this study with my Hollywood congregation, there was a gratifying response to this return to basics. Many people found Christ and began the new life in Him; growing Christians were affirmed and stabilized; and seasoned saints were encouraged by the reminder of the essentials of their faith. People in all three groups joined in the quest for the authentic life.

I want to express my esteem and thankfulness for my administrative assistant, Jeri Gonzalez, who typed the chapters and encouraged the completion of the manuscript. She is the kind of authentic Christian about whom this book is written.

My prayer is that this book will be a source of encouragement, assurance, raw courage, and hope for those who long to live the authentic life in these confusing, pressured times. I believe this will be the most exciting decade for Christians since Pentecost. Now turn to the first chapter and allow me to tell you why.

Lloyd John Ogilvie

1

The Authentic Life

First Thessalonians 1:1

*Grace to you and peace from God our Father
and the Lord Jesus Christ.*

I can't shake it off. I have been given a vision, a hope, an assurance. The Lord has infused me with an exciting dream that this is to be the most dynamic decade since Pentecost. I believe the Lord has placed His hand of blessing back on the institutional church and this will be an unprecedented period of renaissance, new birth, vitality and power. It will be a time in which religious church members find God and are empowered by His Spirit. Lethargic churchmanship will be replaced by contagious Christianity.

Let's face it. In the past decade the Lord has had to bypass the traditional church to get His work done in mission and evangelism. Often the most courageous expressions of adventuresome Christianity were done by the para-church, or completely independent groups which were free to act rather than react to the propitious crises of our time. My analysis of contemporary Christianity reveals that the institutional church has been about five years behind in responding to what God is up to in the world; we retreated in world mission at a time when God was opening up new frontiers for global evangelization. Therefore, new organizations had to be raised up to meet the need. While church committees sat wringing their hands in endless meetings, our Lord was ready to move. Diminished giving to the major denominations caused withdrawal on almost every front; yet, at the same time, giving increased steadily for mission and evangelistic groups with immediacy and freedom to respond to the Lord's call. Independent broadcasters took to the television airwaves and drew off millions in support of their efforts to preach the gospel. Meanwhile, traditional churches sat back wondering where the money went rather than marshalling a media movement of their own. There was not a lack of funds; they were being given to groups people felt were on the move for Christ.

Membership in the major denominations spiraled downward. At the same time Bible-preaching, evangelical churches grew at an unprecedented rate. People gravitated to churches which were alive with biblically-oriented, Christ-centered, Holy Spirit-inspired vitality. Old denominational ties were loosened and pride of heritage was traded for a relevant faith for today's needs.

The traditional church in America faces a crisis of faith. Pastors, church officers, and many members need a penetrating renaissance in which Christ becomes the verve and vitality of a new contagion. We cannot give what we do not have nor reproduce what is not ours. The lack of enthusiasm and spontaneity in many churches has its root in "business as usual" congregational life. The challenge to discipleship is missing. Only when we dare to plan and envision what we could not do on our own strength and resources, do we need to find an intimate relationship with the Lord and become channels of His impossibility-defying, momentous insight. The aching needs of our time demand it; the future of the institutional church requires it.

A study of history gives a perspective. The church has

always been awakened when conditions in society are the bleakest. We are now facing seemingly insolvable problems in our national life and in international affairs. Praise God! Now is when there is a chance for the culturally conditioned institutional church to come alive and confess the subtle syncretism which has infected our life. The church is not the handmaid of culture to assume its humanly-set goals. It is the divine community of God's people, called to model life as it was meant to be. We are to be a sharp contrast, a winsome judgment, and then an agent of renaissance. The local congregation is more than a reflection of culture; it is a band of God's new breed, filled with His Spirit and equipped by the gospel to change lives and confront evil in society.

That presses us to set biblically-rooted goals for the church. Institutions, like individuals, are irrevocably in the process of becoming what they dare to envision. "Without a vision, the people perish" (see Prov. 29:18). If we could set aside all our fears and reservations, what would be our boldest dream for the institutional church in America? Mine is for a dynamic decade of renaissance in which the leaders and members dare to go back to basics. The need of our time is for authentic Christianity to be preached and taught, lived and shared with individuals, and for a radical, to-the-roots quality of discipleship.

And the Lord is doing it! That's the excitement of the vision for this decade which He has given me. I see it happening among denominational leaders, clergy, church officers, and congregations. We are rediscovering the basic meaning of the authentic. The rebirth of intimacy with Christ has its indisputable origin in His initiative invasion of our lives. The newfound excitement about the Lord's power is consistent with the biblical promises. What the Lord did so long ago, He is doing now. And it's congruent with reality. We are daring to listen again to the deepest needs of people and share the liberating power of the gospel to meet those aching voids. Because we are allowing the Lord to deal with our own needs, empathy is replacing aloof sympathy. A faith that was an addendum to our culturally conditioned values, is becoming the essence of a new integrated wholeness around the Lordship of Christ. The world will listen to churches like that. It's happening. A new church in America is being born!

The apostle Paul is our mentor in this new beginning. I am amazed at how that giant of the faith never wandered from basics nor veered off into enticing sidetracks. His message began and ended with two words: grace and peace. The discovery of authentic living is rooted in both. One reveals the nature of our Lord and the other describes the evidence that proves that His nature has been reproduced in us. The one course from which we never graduate is experiencing and communicating grace and peace.

Paul opens his first letter to the Thessalonians with the awesome blessing, "Grace to you and peace from God our Father and the Lord Jesus Christ." The traditional style of beginning a letter in ancient times is used with special care. Paul knew that grace and peace alone had met the emptiness in his own life and that the struggling Christians in Thessalonica could not survive without them. This opening verse of chapter 1 is like a one-theme overture to an opera. And yet, those two words summarized and crystallized everything else Paul would write. The message which had produced new Christians in Thessalonica and gave birth to a vital church was the gospel of grace and peace. The first step to authentic Christianity in our time is to have a fresh, mind-reorienting, character-transplanting, personality-liberating experience of both. The authentic Christians I know who are the firstfruit of a new church for this decade have admitted their ever-increasing need to return to the heart of God for grace and accept the peace which results in their hearts.

If I had to select one word to describe the nature of God it would be *grace.* The word flashes like a diamond held up to the light. It means giving, forgiving, unchanging, unmotivated, unconditional love. God relates to us with accepting and affirming love. The cross is the sublime expression of that unqualified love. Before we were ready, deserving, worthy, Christ died for us.

The apostle Paul never could forget that grace. It was the ethos of his thinking, the ambience of his living, the motivation of his ministry. I am indebted to my New Testament professor, James Stewart of Edinburgh, who helped me discover the key to all of Paul's message. The apostle was a man "in" Christ. The little preposition carries heavy freight. It implies that Paul's intellect, emotions and will were infused by a personal relationship with Christ. He constantly remembered the unlimited grace he experienced on the Damascus Road. His own restless heart was captured by indomitable love. He was transformed from being a persecutor of the faith to becoming its most vigilant proclaimer; from being a self-righteous man to a Christ-reconciled new creation; from hostility toward life to an indefatigable hope. Grace for Paul meant to live in Christ and allow Christ to live in him. One enabled him to receive the blessing of Christ's message, death and resurrection. The other filled his being with the indwelling Christ Himself. The first without the last could not have produced the powerful man Paul became. The secret was that Christ actually took up residence in him.

The greatest need in the church today is for those of us who have believed in Christ to be filled with Him. An authentic person is one who is being transformed into His image. The more we experience His amazing grace, the more we can yield our minds and hearts to be His post-resurrection home. Each of the problems we face are a prelude to fresh grace. They bring us to the end of ourselves and to the place of openness in which He can fill us with Himself. The tissues of our brain can be agents of thinking His thoughts, our emotions can be channels of His warmth and love.

Each time we read the message of grace in the Scriptures, whenever we hear it preached or taught, or when its precious healing balm is offered to us by another who has experienced it afresh, we are given new release and power. Our hunger for grace is never satisfied. God made it so. He created us so that we could live by love alone. Whatever else we accomplish or achieve is empty without it.

Paul learned that repeatedly. The Lord's word to him was, "My grace is sufficient for you, for My strength is made perfect in weakness" (2 Cor. 12:9). The apostle discovered that the Lord Himself was the answer to times of seemingly unanswered prayer. The Lord never gives us anything that will separate us from Him. But there are things which we do that block out our capacity to receive grace.

There is nothing more crippling than our efforts to be adequate on our own strength. After we accept Christ as our Saviour, we often try to live the Christian life *for* Christ rather than *by* His indwelling power. That's the essential cause of the impotence of most Christians and churches today. We soon lose our authenticity in pretense of blind allegiance to traditions, rules or regulations. That puts us on our Damascus Road heading on a collision course with the Saviour. What Paul did with his fanatic zeal for the law, we do for our own self-induced striving to be good enough to be loved for our piety. It is strange how we twist the free gift of grace and try to earn what is ours already!

But the exciting thing I see happening today is that religious people are being set free from that. We are discovering with Paul that Christ's grace is indeed sufficient.

I talked to a pastor of a church in the East. He was bogged down in leading a difficult parish of traditional churchmen and women. I asked him if he could ask for one gift for his people what it would be. His answer was revealing. "I'd ask for what I need as much as they do. An excitement about Christ—a supernatural church in which He is given full reign to change lives and give us the freedom to love and be loved." The response was on target, but required that he begin with himself. We talked for hours about his life. There were memories to be healed, sins to be forgiven, an impossible relationship in his life to be transformed. The man needed to hear the simple message of grace, and experience it in a new way. Our conversation ended on our knees, pouring out to God the emptiness the man felt. Then we prayed to accept the gift of peace for his turbulent heart.

My reason for telling this man's story is because of what happened through him when he returned to his parish. He determined to preach grace for a year. He returned to Christ-centered, cross-oriented preaching. A fire of grace was burning in his own spirit as he talked about the cross, the new life in Christ, the power of the indwelling Christ, and the adventure of being grace-motivated lovers of people. There was boldness, freedom, joy. One by one his officers joined him in his search for authentic Christianity. Then the fire of Pentecost began to spread throughout the congregation. It is now part of Christ's new church for a decade of renaissance!

I talk to members of the laity everywhere who have found new life in Christ by submitting their fears and failures to His grace. Recently a woman said, "I've been a church member for years, but it wasn't until my arrogant religiosity was broken by an unsolvable problem in a relationship with my son that I had to go back to the cross for grace to sustain me. It's amazing! The basic message that Christ loves me and can take the broken pieces of this mess and make something out of it gave me hope and peace." The great thing about this woman's recovery of grace is that once she surrendered her need and saw Christ at work, she became a very gracious person. The Lord has used her repeatedly in helping others with similar problems. Her self-satisfied, aloof judgmentalism was transformed by grace.

I know grace in my own life. My experience of Christ began when friends explained to me the wonder of His grace. My whole Christian experience through 32 years of knowing the Saviour has been a never-ending growth in grace. Some time during each day I am brought back to the fact of the cross. I can readily agree with Charles G. Finney, "A state of mind that sees God in everything is evidence of growth in grace and a thankful heart."

Paul began his first letter to the Thessalonians where the search for the authentic begins and never ends: grace. It is the most significant single word which unlocks the secret of the apostle's immense power and effectiveness. He would have agreed with Robert Louis Stevenson, "There is nothing but God's grace. We walk upon it; we breathe it; we live and die by it; it makes the nails and axles of the universe."

It was the preaching of grace which began authentic Christianity in Thessalonica. Paul knew that the troubles the new Christians were having would be an occasion for a deeper experience of this grace.

Peace is the result of the consistent realization of grace. Peace is not the absence of difficulty, it is the result of grace in difficulty. When we know that we are loved to the uttermost, we can remain peaceful in all of the anxiety life dishes out. Paul has a great deal to say about peace throughout his Epistles. For him, it was the by-product of forgiveness. The Lord took the broken pieces of his troubled heart and gave him peace. He never got over the joy of that. Throughout his ministry he preached that reality. Peace had been made through the blood of the cross (see Col. 1:20). Those who would accept that grace would know a peace which would rule in their hearts (see Col. 3:15) and would guard their hearts from anxiety (see Phil. 4:7). Paul offered the Thessalonians the gift they needed to live the authentic life: grace motivated peace. Accepting the gift would mean inner calm in conflict and unity in the fellowship.

Today our world longs for peace and is more hopeless about discovering it than ever before. All of the international crises indicate that this will be one of the most troubled decades in centuries. This can be the Christian's finest hour! The Lord has given us the answer to how to find peace. But once again we are reminded that we can give away only what we have.

Our church in Hollywood receives a large number of new members each month. I am always delighted when the new people witness that it was the quality of authentic peace in someone in the congregation that attracted them to our church. The most magnetic attraction of our church is in the way our people express peace in life's problems. People today need exactly what Paul preached and modeled there in Thessalonica.

The indisputable origin of the authentic Christian life is in the essential gift of grace and peace. This is the source of the genuine new life we will talk about as we move through the major themes of Paul's letters to the Thessalonians. Everything we will discover is dependent on this two-part blessing.

We can all share in what God is doing in this decade of renaissance. The only qualification is that we be open receivers. What in your life presses you back to grace as your only sufficiency? The sure test that you have allowed God to give you His grace is that, right now, there is an abiding peace which nothing or no one can destroy.

2

U-Turn Absolutely Required!

First Thessalonians 1:2-10

*You turned to God from idols to serve
the living and true God.*

As I drove a rented car in a strange city searching for a church where I was to speak, I suddenly realized I had passed the address and was heading in the wrong direction. I tried to turn around but each intersection had a large "No U-Turn" sign. Irritated, I finally turned off the thoroughfare and headed down a side street hoping to be able to double back. It was a cul-de-sac with a large traffic sign which read just the opposite of the ones which had kept me moving away from my destination. This one, obviously painted by residents who wanted to maintain the privacy of their dead-end street, boldly proclaimed, "U-Turn Absolutely Required!" My frustration was replaced with delight. I had experienced a contemporary parable.

The Christian life begins with an authentic conversion. The word "conversion" means to turn around. A U-turn is absolutely required. Rather than running away from God in willful independence, we can turn around and move toward Him in response to His outstretched arms of love, forgiveness, grace and peace. An authentic conversion, in the context of our definition of authentic, is of undisputed origin, genuine, trustworthy, certain, current, verifiable, true and sure. A decisive U-turn is in response to God's call. It is a real about-face; it changes the total direction of our lives and stands the test of time.

The great need today is for the conversion of religious people who, though they believe in God, are heading away from Him and not to Him. Many church people are trying to live a life they have never begun. I said that at a conference of church leaders recently. I was surprised, and then alarmed, by how many agreed. Some told me of their own traumatic conversions after some years in the church and the ministry. Others shared the stories of members of their churches who were completely turned around through a personal, fresh experience of God's grace and a complete surrender of their lives to His guidance and power.

The most satisfying thing I see happening today in the new renaissance in the church we talked about in the previous chapter, is that people who had drifted into the church with a vague half-belief, are experiencing an authentic conversion. Beyond a generalized hunch, they are finding hope; more than ideas about God, they are discovering intimacy with Him; instead of running away from God, they are allowing Him to run their lives. The authentic is replacing the apocryphal. A new church is being born in our time! It is made up of soundly converted people who have made a U-turn that is genuine. What happened in Thessalonica so long ago is happening today. That's why a study of Paul's letters to the infant church there is so crucial. We are called back to essentials. Like those new Christians, we need to be assured and affirmed in the triumphant turnaround Christ has accomplished in our lives.

After Paul's opening greeting, he launches into thanksgiving for the authentic conversion of the Thessalonian Christians. Verse 2 to the end of the chapter is an unstudied rush of rhetoric tumbling forth from the apostle's grateful heart. What had happened to him on the Damascus Road had been reproduced in the lives of people he had grown to love. Each person's experience had been a unique expression of his or her individuality. And yet, in all of them there had been an indisputable turning point that was decisive and definite. Now they needed to know that Paul knew and thanked God for what had happened to them.

The key to unfolding the unpolished structure of this first chapter is in verse 9: "You turned to God from idols to serve the living and true God." The word for "turned" in the Greek is *epistrephō,* the same word used for conversion throughout the New Testament.

The church was made up of Jews from the synagogue, Greeks from the busy commercial city, and Romans stationed there by Emperor Claudius. The church represented the religious, the philosophical intellectuals and the materialists of every age who needed conversion from idols to the true and living God. The Jews had their idols of the law, rules, regulations, customs and traditions. The Greeks had their Parthenon of gods for all seasons. The Romans had their Caesar worship and an imperious lust for power. And Paul strode into their city with a gospel that met the deepest need of all three groups. He preached that Jesus was the Messiah, that His death on the cross was the once, never-to-be-repeated atonement for the sins of the world, and that He was alive with them there in Thessalonica to love, forgive and empower. Not one more god, not another religion, not an added compulsion, but an impelling offer of abundant life in Christ and Christ in them. The apostle's preaching secured a beachhead in Europe by the birth of a profoundly converted church. It was a fellowship of turned-around people.

In these nine verses of chapter 1, Paul gives us a comprehensive compilation of the meaning of conversion. The more I have studied this affirmation of the turning point of the Thessalonians, the more I have realized that the nine elements of an authentic conversion are given to us. They provide an incisive inventory of the genuineness of our own conversion. They afford both comfort and challenge. A sharp edge is given us on which to cut through to the reality of the extent of our own U-turn. The nine dimensions can be divided into three triplets, each containing three aspects of the transforming turning point. Paul tells us what God does, what happens to us, and then what happens through us. All are strategic and inseparably related to the others.

Consider first what God did among the Thessalonians and wants to do in us today. The first triplet is made up of (1) election, (2) the power of the Holy Spirit and (3) assurance. An authentic conversion begins with God's gift of calling, confrontation and confirmation.

The context of this first triplet in verses 4 and 5 is communicated by a very special name by which Paul calls the Thessalonians: beloved brethren. Previously this sacred designation had been used only for the great men of Israel's history or for the nation of Israel herself. It means beloved by God. Now it is extended to the heterogeneous fellowship of Jews, Greeks and Romans, men and women of the church of Thessalonica! The grace of God had broken the religious, social, cultural, economic and sexist barriers. The searching, yearning, pursuing heart of God is where conversion begins. And that heart of unlimited love is Christ, Emmanuel, God with us. He came and comes. He is the "hound of heaven" to use Francis Thompson's image, who tracks us indefatigably.

The first step in our conversion is election: "Knowing, beloved brethren, your election by God" (v. 4). Jesus tells us what He told the disciples, "You have not chosen Me, but I have chosen you" (John 15:16). By the mystery of election we are the called, appointed, chosen people of the Lord. The undisputed origin of an authentic conversion is in that choice. It is not based on our achievement, adequacy, excellence or exemplary life.

The Lord constantly calls impossible people to do the impossible. The Scriptures are filled with examples of people like Abraham, Moses, Gideon, David, Peter, Mark, or Paul who were called not because of their credentials but because of the Lord's plan for them. A sure sign of our election is our amazement that He should choose us. If we think we have been chosen as the best of men and women because of our stellar character or impeccable performance, we have missed the divine origin of our election.

Paul constantly was astounded that the Lord had elected him. After all that he had done and been, His call was a source of humbling delight. Later in Paul's ministry he polished his convictions about election into a more clearly defined theological statement. He wrote to the Christians at Rome, "And we know that all things work together for good to those who love God, to those who are the called according to His purpose. For whom He foreknew, He also predestined to be conformed to the image of His Son, that He might be the firstborn among many brethren. Moreover whom He predestined, these He also called; whom He called, these He also justified; and whom He justified, these He also glorified" (Rom. 8:28-30). This is an excellent description of the source, substance and sublimity of conversion. Note the progression: God's foreknowledge, election, calling, justification through forgiveness and reconciliation, and then glorification by making us like Christ. Conversion is the process by which we are reformed into the image of Christ. And it all begins in knowing that we did not choose, but were chosen.

Do you know that for yourself? Is the most sure and solid reality of your life the knowledge that you belong to God, that you are beloved, cherished, and that He has invaded your life with an undeniable call to turn around and come to Him? Clarence Macartney was right, "God's favorite word is—come!"

This leads us to the second part of this first triad. *The*

Holy Spirit, Christ with us, is the one who delivers the call, makes it undeniably clear, excavates a sense of need, and convinces us that what was accomplished on Calvary is for each of us. Paul wanted the Thessalonians to be sure of the Lord's clarion voice which had sounded in their souls: "For our gospel did not come to you in word only, but also in power, in the Holy Spirit" (I Thess. 1:5). In the din of the many voices calling for an allegiance, the voice of the Lord rises above all the rest. He comes to us so that we can respond to His "come unto me." He will use everything happening to and around us to bring us to the end of our own resources and to the beginning of a new life. Conversion is the work of the living Christ, the power of the Holy Spirit. He uses the two powerful weapons He used with the Thessalonians: the communication of the gospel and the example of the communicator. Paul speaks of "our gospel" and "what kind of men we were among you *for your sake*" (italics added).

The dynamic combination which brings us to the need of conversion is the clear, clean and undiluted identification of our plight and Christ's power, communicated by a person who speaks with the authenticity of personal experience and living. My own conversion began by meeting a couple of people who shared the gospel and gave me an example of what Christ could do with a life completely surrendered to Him. When I got down on my knees in a college dormitory, over 30 years ago, and accepted my call to be Christ's man, it was because for the first time I experienced truth explained and exemplified. The Holy Spirit convinced me that I was heading in the wrong direction. My turnaround, U-turn, was enabled by vivid examples in people of what I could become if I allowed Christ to love me.

This happened to me and countless millions of others throughout 20 centuries because of what Paul calls *"much assurance," the third part of this triad.* This is the personal conviction that we are loved unconditionally, forgiven unreservedly, and accepted unqualifiedly. We are assured that we belong to Christ and nothing can ever change that fact. This third aspect of what He does to launch our conversion gives us the courage of Hebrews 10:22,23, "Let us draw near with a true heart in full assurance of faith, having our hearts sprinkled from an evil conscience and our bodies washed with pure water. Let us hold fast the confession of our hope without wavering, for He who promised is faithful."

Assurance is to be sure we are secure, to know that we are known. It is the full confidence which makes us Christ-confident people. The Greek word Paul uses here for "assurance" is *plērophoriāi.* He also uses it in Colossians 2:2, expressing his hope for beloved friends, "that their hearts may be encouraged, being knit together in love, and attaining to all riches of the full *assurance* of understanding, to the knowledge of the mystery of God" (italics added). H. A. Ironside put it succinctly: "Faith rests on the naked Word of God; that Word believed gives full assurance."

Let me recap the three keys of this first tripod of conversion. The sure foundation of a true U-turn is our (1) election issuing in an undeniable call, (2) the work of the Holy Spirit convincing us of our need and the gospel's truth, and (3) inner assurance that we are accepted in spite of all we know about ourselves that is unacceptable. Without that there is no beginning, but if that's the end of it, we have not really begun. So let's press on to the second triplet. It explains what changes in us when we know that we are chosen, called and assured by sheer grace.

This second triplet is found in verse 3 of Paul's thanksgiving, "Remembering without ceasing your work of faith, labor of love, and patience of hope." The three dimensions of the result of conversion in us are (1) faith, (2) love, and (3) hope.

Faith is a gift. It is the primary endowment of the Spirit. He alone can give us the power to respond to the gospel. So often we think of faith as something we produce. Not so. Faith is an imputed capacity to accept the fact that Christ died for us and that we are His called and cherished persons.

Faith is the Lord's implanted seed. All we can do is offer the fertile soil of openness and willingness. Faith lodges in our minds and hearts and sends down radical rootlets into the totality of our nature. Authentic conversion is radical "to the roots." It is penetrating to the core of our nature. A deeply-rooted faith transforms our character around absolute allegiance to Christ. Then our goals, values, and desires are completely reoriented.

Faith enables us to trust our lives, now and forever, to the gracious providence of God. That is what enabled Paul to say, "For I am not ashamed of the gospel of Christ, for it is the power of God to salvation for everyone who believes . . . for in it the righteousness of God is revealed from faith to faith; as it is written, 'The just shall live by faith' " (Rom. 1:16,17). To this Luther added "Sola!"

The just shall live by faith *alone!* "For by grace you have been saved through faith, and that not of yourselves; it is the gift of God, not of works, lest anyone should boast" (Eph. 2:8,9). Thus we see that authentic faith has its origins in the Spirit's work in us. It is genuine when it is no replica of anyone else's faith or a facsimile produced by our effort. True faith gives us the power to surrender our minds, hearts and wills to our Lord. We invite Him to control all our affairs. Then we relinquish our self-will to do His will. As Thoreau put it: "We march to a different drummer."

The result of faith is love. The rootlets of a radical faith send up the strong stem of love piercing through the layers of our reserve and expressing the beauty of full-blossomed love in action and expression. Love too is a gift. The Holy Spirit is love. When He dwells in us we are able to love as we've been loved. We reach out with caring, involvement, initiative forgiveness and acceptance. A radical U-turn always results in a new power to love. It can safely be said that if we are not filled with love for people, we are probably not converted. If our minds are still poisoned with negative judgments and censorious criticism, we have had an incomplete turning point.

A man who became a Christian recently exclaimed, "I am amazed. I thought I would have to try to love to assure my conversion. But instead I am sure of my conversion by the fact that I am able to do and say loving things that before would have been completely foreign to my nature. The other day I read an explanation in 2 Corinthians 5:17 of what's happening to me. Listen to this! [He was excited to share that he had memorized the verse]. 'Therefore, if anyone is in Christ, he is a new creation; old things have passed away; behold, all things have become new.' "

Paul talks about the "labor" of love evidenced in the Thessalonians. The word does not mean effort. The sure test of our conversion is spontaneous love. It doesn't have to be plotted or planned. It flows naturally from being loved. Nothing is more convincing to others that we've turned around than the warmth of costly love they feel in our presence.

The third part of this second triplet of conversion is *"patience of hope in our Lord Jesus Christ."* A faith that is radical produces love that is undeniable and issues in a hope that is indomitable. But be sure to note that this hope resulting from conversion is in our Lord Jesus Christ. All other hopes are fleeting and eventually disappointing. As we will note in chapter 5, Paul's hope was based in what Christ did, does and will do in His second coming. Christian hope is grounded in the Resurrection. Christ's resurrection reminds us that God can take the worst and give His best. Our own resurrection from death to self to a deathless life gives us courage to face life's problems and disappointments with the sure conviction that our Lord will intervene and infuse His power. We can face anything with that assurance.

In this dynamic decade of the Lord's blessing on the church, hope will be our banner. As the world becomes more confused, we will become more confident; as man's efforts plunge us deeper into world catastrophe, the fellowship of God's people will become even more triumphant in the conviction that nothing can separate us from His love. Remember the promise: when world conditions become worse the condition of the church will be stronger!

Hope provides patience. We are able to take the long view of things. The shortness of history and the length of eternity give us patience with the trifles of life. Hope provides the perspective of true patience. A truly converted person knows he belongs to Christ. His nature is being reproduced in him. Patience was surely an attribute of Jesus of Nazareth. Picture what He would do in life's pressures when you are tempted to be impatient. That's exactly what He will do through you. What a remarkable way to live!

Now we are ready to consider the third triplet. As a result of what the Lord did for and in the Thessalonians, they were enabled to do three things. They (1) became followers of the Lord, (2) knew joy in affliction, and (3) became examples to others. Authentic conversion is manifested in these sure signs of discipleship.

The Greek word for "followers" is *mimēsthai* from *mimeomai*, to imitate. Pauls says that *the Thessalonians became imitators of him*, Timothy and Silas, and most of all, of the Lord. Thomas á Kempis described true discipleship as "the imitation of Christ." Once we've made a U-turn, the passion of our lives is to live and act like Christ.

During the long days and nights of my study time in Thessalonica (modern Thessaloniki) I had ample time to reflect on each of the verses of Paul's Thessalonian letters. No verse hit me harder than this one. To what an extent am I a *mimēsthai* of Christ? That led to a profound inventory of my life, values, priorities, goals. As a result of one day's silence on this verse alone, I felt a recall to be a follower. Nothing could be placed in the way of that.

I walked back and forth on the wharf for hours asking the Lord for fresh guidance on how I could follow Him, be like Him more faithfully. At the end of the day I wrote down what He gave me. I refer to it often. What do you think the Lord would say to you if you allowed Him to talk to you on that one subject for a full day? Try it!

But there is something more in this verse. Paul commended the Thessalonians on the fact that they had also become followers of him and his missionary band. That leads us to wonder about the impact of our lives on others. We reproduce ourselves; we cannot lead anyone any further than we have dared to grow ourselves. People around us are taking signals all the time from our actions and reactions. I think of the thousands of people I've met over the years who will not take the gospel seriously because of what they experienced of Christianity in their homes or some local church. That's no excuse to be sure, but the negative example has had its toll.

I often think of the question asked of a congregation in an installation service for a pastor or church officers: "Will you follow this person insofar as he follows Christ?" There's the crucial issue! The Thessalonians would have been able to say an enthusiastic "Yes!" if that question had been asked them about Paul.

When people in our church in Hollywood are asked to prayerfully consider becoming church elders, they must agree to several challenges.

1. *Faith:* Are you unreservedly committed to Christ as Saviour and Lord? Do you have complete trust in Him as indwelling power and head of the church?

2. *Freedom:* Has your faith issued in freedom to allow the Lord to love you, love yourself, and give yourself away to others? Do you have an openness to receive His guidance and follow Him obediently? Are you free to lead others to Christ and care for them as they grow as Christians?

3. *Fellowship:* Are you willing to allow the Session to be a church in miniature, modeling to the congregation what the church as a whole is meant to be? (The Session is the ruling body in a Presbyterian church.) Will you enter into the prayer and study, love and concern of the fellowship so that the Session may be the beloved community? There must be an

implosion of spiritual power among the officers before there is an explosion of new life in the congregation.

4. *Finances:* Are you willing to be a biblical Christian in your giving, tithing 10 percent of your income, becoming a courageous, exemplary giver?

5. *Follow-through:* Are you willing to be an "initiative implementor," following the guidance of our Lord in the program He has led the Session to adopt according to ten-, five-, three-, and one-year goals?

The significant thing about this inventory is that it develops a core of spiritual adventurers boldly leading the congregation. A local church will move as fast and as far as the officers have discovered individually and lived out in their life together. A new church for this decade is dependent on a new breed of lay leaders whom people can follow. They must be responsive to the Holy Spirit, reproductive in communicating their faith to others, radical in pressing the congregation ahead in the Lord's goals, and reconciling agents in maintaining the peace and unity of the church.

Often it is in challenges and difficulties that our faith has its greatest impact on others. Paul commended the Thessalonians for the second part of this third triad. They had *the joy of the Holy Spirit in much affliction.* An authentic conversion is verified by how we do in life's tight places. The acid test of our turning around in a complete conversion is how we live our faith in the testing times. The new church in Thessalonica needed Paul's affirmation of their courage to stand fast in the Lord in spite of harsh blasts of criticism and hostility they were receiving from all sides. The Jews in the synagogues opposed them, the Greeks ridiculed them, the Romans resisted them. These new Christians were an unsettling contradiction of life in Thessalonica.

Joy is the outward expression of the inner experience of grace. It is so much more than happiness which is dependent on circumstances. True joy results from the confidence that the Lord will see us through and that He will never leave or forsake us. We can say with the psalmist, "Many are the afflictions of the righteous; but the Lord delivers him out of them all" (Ps. 34:19).

This is intertwined with the last aspect of authentic conversion. *We will have an infectious influence.* Paul complimented the Thessalonians on the example they had become to all in Macedonia and Achaia: "For from you the word of the Lord has sounded forth, not only in Macedonia and Achaia, but also in every place your faith toward God has gone out, so that we do not need to say anything" (1 Thess. 1:8). The Greek word for "sounded forth" is *exēchētai* from *exēcheō,* to sound out like a trumpet or thunder, or to reverberate like an echo; the dynamic power of influence.

These Thessalonians were the trumpet of the Lord. That reminds us of what happened to Gideon when the Spirit of the Lord took possession of him. "So the Spirit of the Lord came upon Gideon; and he blew a trumpet" (Judg. 6:34). The actual Hebrew of that verse is "The Spirit of the Lord clothed Himself with Gideon and he blew the trumpet." This is what happened to those strategically located new Christians in Thessalonica. Think of it! In a few months news of their conversion spread to the then known world. Travelers on the Roman road carried the news; sailors from the harbor city gossiped about the gospel. The Lord is an excellent strategist. By establishing a vital church in Thessalonica, His message of new life spread like wildfire. Eventually the evangelization of Europe would result.

The same is true for each of us, and our task is to be faithful. The Lord does the rest. He puts us in touch with people and situations He wants to reach. None of us will ever know until we get to heaven how many people were influenced by us or by people we helped into the adventure of the new life.

An authentic conversion will result in the conversion of others. It is safe to say that we have not experienced a U-turn unless we can identify people we have influenced for Christ by our witness, and helped them through the steps of conversion. All the techniques of evangelism, devised with mass meetings and programs, will never substitute for the one-to-one influence on others which the radically converted Christian exerts. It is every Christian's birthright to be a reproducer. The untapped reservoir for the evangelization of the world is the contagious believer. Our challenge is to discover a winsome way of sharing our faith that works for us.

I am convinced that if each of us lived our faith with "all-stops-out" enthusiasm, and were willing to talk about what Christ means to us in the pressures of life, we would have more opportunities to help others find a personal relationship with Christ than we ever imagined. But that requires an assurance of our own conversion and a clarity of explaining it to others. That's why a deep study of this first chapter of Thessalonians is so helpful. We can move back through the nine steps of conversion, be sure each has happened to us and then be ready to lead others through them in their quest for authentic conversion. When we "turn from idols to serve the living true God," that service will primarily be helping others find the eternal life we have experienced.

In communicating the faith, utilize these nine crucial steps:

1. Help people know that they are elected, called, chosen. No one longs to find God who has not first been found by Him.

2. Explain the simple promises of the gospel with the confidence that the Holy Spirit is at work in minds and hearts creating receptivity and openness. Tell them God loves them. Share the profound meaning of the cross for their forgiveness and reconciliation. Communicate the secret that to love God is to allow Him to love them.

3. Assure them that God's love will never let them go. They belong to Him, now and for eternity.

4. Enable them to accept the gift of faith from the Holy

Spirit to appropriate all that was done for them on Calvary and surrender all of the past, present and future to Him.

5. Affirm the new love for God, self and others which begins to flow in a person as the evidence that the Lord has taken up residence in him or her. Help the new convert to be to others what Christ has been to him or her. Help the person do a relational inventory. Whom does he need to forgive; whose forgiveness should he seek? What restitution for past sin needs to be done? Love wipes the slate clean so we can live with freedom.

6. Show from your own life how hope in Christ has worked for you and can work for him or her in all of life's challenges and opportunities. Encourage the person to commit all the uncertainties and problems to Him, expecting His intervention.

7. Stay in touch with the person until he or she becomes a follower of the Lord. That means discovering the power of prayer for guidance in all of life's decisions and needs. An intimate companionship with the Master is the essence of the Christian life.

8. Encourage the joy the Lord gives in affliction. It will come as the person sorts out the implications of obedience to Christ. Help maximize the joy the Lord provides in the times of testing. Be an encourager.

9. Become a strategist in helping the person discover the power of his or her influence. Our work is not finished until the person has led another person to Christ. Help him to become aware of people's need for what has happened to him. We can keep only what we give away! You will have helped a person live life as it was meant to be.

If we are to cooperate with what God wants to do in this dynamic decade, a U-turn is absolutely required—in each of us and then through us in others. Check the nine steps Paul has given us. Are they all real for you? Have they happened in your life? Everything else the Lord longs to give us is dependent on a complete turn-around, an authentic conversion.

3

Love As It Was Meant to Be

First Thessalonians 2

*That you would walk worthy of God who calls
you into His own kingdom and glory.*

Every one of us has three things in common. We need to be loved, we need to learn how to love, and we have people in our lives who desperately need our love. The essence of life is love. Giving and receiving love. Being loved and loving is the foundation and sublime expression of authentic living. Henry Drummond was right, "Love is the greatest thing in the world." The evidence that we've had an authentic turning point is that we become recipients of a liberating love and become creative lovers of others.

Chapter 2 of Paul's first letter to the Thessalonians is a hymn to love though the word is never mentioned. Once again our working definition of *authentic* serves to give us an outline of our thought. The love Paul felt and expressed in this chapter is of undisputed origin; it was original, genuine, congruent, and current. As we follow the flow of his thought, we are exposed to love as it was meant to be. Three things grip us as we read this unashamed expression of love: it shows us Paul's freedom to love, reminds us of how he loved the Thessalonians when he was with them, and gives us a guide to learn how to love profoundly today.

As we have noted before, each of the passages in the Thessalonian letters has a jugular vein, a key verse which unlocks the meaning of the whole section of the letter. For me, verse 12 of this second chapter is the port of entry to the apostle's thought. "That you would walk worthy of God who calls you into His own kingdom and glory." The word *worthy* is the live wire of the verse. It gives an electrifying insight not only to this strategic verse, but also to the whole passage. The word is *axiōs* in Greek. It means weight and comes from the realm of weights and measures. An *axiōs* is the measure which balances the scale.

Picture a scale with one empty bowl on each side. They are perfectly balanced, ready for the weight to be placed on one side to be balanced by the contents of the other side.

Now on one side place Christ's love and what it means to you. Begin with His ministry as Saviour and Lord. Consider how He has dealt with you just as He reached out and cared for individuals during His brief incarnation. Next contemplate His death and what that means for your forgiveness, reconciliation and freedom from guilt and self-condemnation. Now pile onto the scale Pentecost and the Lord's return through the Holy Spirit to indwell you with power. Add to that the precious weight of His daily intervention and momentary guidance. Look at the scales tip!

Next place your own life and your efforts to love on the other side. Think about your relationships. The people whom you have tried to love and need to love. Reflect on the ones who need unmerited forgiveness and uncalculating assurance. We can hardly budge the scale to any modicum of balance. How can we ever thank the Lord enough for what He's done and does for us?

Paul's admonition to walk worthy of God is staggering. The term "walk" is a Pauline metaphor for living. How can we ever live a life which in any way is a balance to what Christ exemplified? We can't without His indwelling Spirit. He presses us on to love in His style and by His power. The indisputable origin of authentic love is in the quality of the Lord's love for us. Have we persisted in loving as He persists indefatigably with us? The love we need for others is Christ Himself invading our hearts and expressing Himself through us. That's the secret of balancing the scale. Let Him do it!

This is what happened to the apostle Paul. It was not only the love he had experienced on the Damascus Road, or in his time of preparation for ministry, it was a constantly renewed love from Christ pouring through the open channel in his heart.

In the light of our understanding of the fulcrum of verse 12, we can move back to the opening of chapter 2 and discover the crucial elements of authentic love.

The first thing we discover about this quality of love from verses 1 through 6 is that it is not dependent on people. *True love is original in its source.* And the origin is Christ. The love Paul communicated was of the kind that the world could neither give nor take away. It was the manifestation of an intimate companionship with Christ. Outflow was directly proportionate to inflow. Fear was constantly replaced by courage, hostility by compassion, defensiveness by involvement.

Note what Christ's love in him endured in Paul's Macedonian ministry. He suffered and was mistreated in Philippi. Imprisonment and persecution did not diminish his love. He had boldness to speak the gospel amid opposition. His love was not dependent on the people and their response. There was no quid pro quo of bartered affection. The apostle was not balancing a scale weighted with people's approbation, but one loaded with the Lord's grace. He was free to love in spite of what people said and did.

Allow the full impact of this to stir your soul. After Philippi Paul did not need a long period to be healed of the rejection. Instead he strode over the mountains and began all over again in Thessalonica. He did not project onto the Thessalonians the bruises of a dejected spirit. Not for a moment did he take out on the Thessalonians what the officialdom of Philippi had done to him. He was able to close one chapter and begin the next. Shaking the dust off his feet, he pressed on.

That's not easy. So often we allow our minds to brood over previous slights and oversights, hurts and diminished hopes. A protective membrane is formed over our hearts so we will never be bothered by rejection again. And when we are, the membrane thickens until we become incapable of warmth and love.

The other day a man said, "I just can't love anymore. I've had it! Do to others what you want them to do to you? That Golden Rule is tarnished and rusted. It doesn't work. I try to love and it's not returned. I give up!" The reason for his exaggeration was that he had loved to be loved. That's not Christian love as Paul modeled it.

The point is that we can't really love people as long as we need them. Most of the times when we say "I love you" we are saying "I desperately need you!" Whenever we love in order to assure a return of love, we are disappointed. The reason is that no one can love us as much as we need to be loved. Only Christ can do that! If we try to manipulate from another person what we were meant to receive from Him, we will create an idol who will eventually fall from his or her pedestal.

Paul didn't need the Thessalonians. All he needed was Christ. That freed him to be one of the most courageous lovers of all time. That's what he meant when he wrote, "For our exhortation did not come from deceit or uncleanness, nor was it in guile" (v. 3). He did not need to manipulate a loving response from his new friends by clever devices. The reason is given us in verse 4. The Lord's approval was all that was important. "But as we have been approved by God to be entrusted with the gospel, even so we speak, not as pleasing men, but God who tests our hearts."

Original love from the Lord frees us from the endless effort to please people. When we know that He is pleased with us in spite of what we've been or done, that He offers forgiveness and a million new beginnings, we can get out of the sick syndrome of trying to please the people around us. Love impels us to say and do the things people need, but not just what a whim wants. People can play us like yo-yos in an endless up and down, alternating emotional highs and lows, if we are dependent on their fluctuating emotions. Courageous loving is rooted in the constancy of Christ's love. His love never fails!

Perhaps you are in one of those slumps right now depending on people's response to you more than on the assurance of Christ's "I'll-never-let-you-go" quality of love. It happens to all of us. We can all remember times when we were hurt so badly that we question whether we want to try to love again.

I talked to a fellow pastor recently who confessed his anxious dependence on his congregation's approval and approbation. He said, "I'm like an actor I know who waits around by the stage door for hours, talking to people, desperately in need of being told he's great. The only difference for me is that I greet my congregation after a service anxiously awaiting the 'great sermon, you're super' responses."

The remarkable thing about this man is how much he keeps telling his people that he loves them. He's discovered that his eloquent protestation is advertising his need. He says I love you to assure the same from his people. That insecurity has taken the cutting edge out of his preaching and leadership. He avoids confrontation and adjusts his message so he will never offend. But the result was mirrored in his face. There was an equivocation in his expression, a shifting of his eyes. Solicitousness showed from his body language. Soon he became anxious, a telltale sign of suppressed anger. No longer could he say with Paul, "not as pleasing men, but God." It has taken a long time and penetrating fellowship with this man to recover the prophet buried in his soul.

Often we inherit the "if-you-love-me-you-will-do-what-pleases-me" syndrome from parents who use it as the only way to get or keep children in line. We end up playing games all through our lives.

We need to take a page from Paul's manual for creative relationships. "For neither at any time did we use flattering words, as you know, nor a cloak for covetousness—God is witness. Nor did we seek glory from men, neither from you nor from others" (vv. 5,6). The indwelling love of Christ makes us honest, direct, decisive. Authentic love wills the ultimate good of others and takes the initiative steps toward this end. Words and actions of love are expressed by the impelling motive power of Christ's love. We can give ourselves away recklessly for people's needs without needing them. People will know and feel they are loved. We will ring true in our relationship with them. They will know that they are valued, esteemed, cherished and that we are willing to live or die for them. I'll never forget a visit of Frank Laubach to our home years ago. He was a man who loved profoundly. He once said, "When iron is rubbed against a magnet, it becomes magnetic. Just so, love is caught, not taught. One heart burning with love sets another on fire. The church was built on love; it proves what love can do."

Paul's love for the Thessalonians proved what love can do. It was not only original love from the undisputed origin of Christ Himself, it was a love distinguished by the next aspect of the authentic. *It was genuine.* In the seventh and eleventh verses of chapter 2 we are given two inseparable dimensions of genuine love. "We were gentle among you, just as a nursing mother cherishes her own children . . . as you know how we exhorted, comforted, and charged every one of you, as a father does his own children." Here are two powerful dynamics of what it means to love a person.

The image of a mother nursing her child is vivid. It means

a mother breast-feeding her child. Latent memory feelings are stirred from our inner being and a picture of tenderness forms in our minds. A nursing mother gives of her own sustenance. A part of her passes from her life-giving breast to a hungry suckling. Paul's metaphor is deeply moving. Our love for people is to be that same kind of self-sacrificial giving of ourselves. No mother feeds a child from her breast grudgingly or reluctantly. That's the essence of authentic love.

I remember a cross-Atlantic flight from London to New York on a British Airways jet. I was crammed into a no-frills economy section seat with an English engineer and a mother holding a squalling infant. The child cried incessantly for hours, upsetting all the passengers. He was hungry and the more he cried the more embarrassed the mother became. Tension bordered on pain on her face. Seated between two men, she was not about to breast-feed her distraught child. Looking back on the event, I can't imagine why the two of us were so insensitive and involved in our work that we missed what was the need of this child and the frustration of his sweet young mother. I was trying to finish up some work before arriving in New York and was acting like a typical male who had forgotten how his own three children had been fed in infancy.

Finally, after hours of anguished crying, a woman British army officer came marching down the aisle of the plane with a blanket tucked under her arm. She was like one of those imposing, commanding women who have built and maintained the British Empire—broad-shouldered, wide-heeled shoes, tailored uniform that made you want to salute, and the officious mannerisms of a sergeant-major! Here was a kind of woman who could drive a general's command car, organize the frightened people in a bomb shelter or marshall a relief movement following a catastrophe. A special breed, indeed! She strode up with purpose in her firmly-set jaw, looking at the engineer and me with impatience and urgency. Her British accent cracked out orders to both of us. "You two—get out of there! Stop your work and move to another seat."

"Yes ma'am!" I returned, moving as fast as I could to a seat she had arranged.

Then she took the blanket and folded it around the frightened mother and her famished child. Her voice softened as she said, "Alright now, with those chaps out of the way, do what you've got to do!" Immediately the child's crying was replaced with satisfied sounds of contentment. The whole section of the plane relaxed with a smile of understanding. The tenderness of what was happening pervaded all of us, including the army officer, who tried to hide her empathy behind her crusty face.

The incident came back to me as I contemplated what Paul communicated about his love for the Thessalonians. He could not have selected a more emotional expression. He had nursed the spiritual infants of Thessalonica with immense care. His tenderness had been given without limit to these babes in Christ as they were fed with the elemental milk of the gospel of Christ's love, forgiveness and assurance. Their turn-around had resulted in their being born again and they needed encouragement.

Tenderness is basic to all our relationships. People never outgrow their need for it. We know that from our own lives. We all need people who are for us, who understand, who listen and empathize patiently and who enter into our joy and pain with identification and compassion. How can we give less to other people than what we constantly expect from them and our Lord?

An examination of the Greek of verse 7 gives us further insight about how to develop this quality of love. The phrase, "We were gentle among you," opens the deeper meaning of "as a nursing mother cherishes . . . " There is a sudden shift in metaphors from gentle to nursing mother. Textual analysis has produced a sharp difference between scholars over the word translated in the English text as "gentle." Some ancient Greek manuscripts contain *ēpioi,* "gentle," while others have *nēpioi,* "babes." The word "became," *egenēthē-men,* which precedes it ends with the letter *n.* It is easy to see how the two renderings—babes or gentle—differing only by the presence or absence of the letter *n* may have happened. Nestle's *Novum Testamentum Graece* has *ēpioi* with appropriate footnotes acknowledging the alternative in other manuscripts. We are left to decide. The *New American Standard Bible,* the *New King James Bible* and the *New English Bible* as well as the authorized *King James Version* all use "gentle."

It is intriguing to consider the implications of both alternatives and then see how either could have been a part of the apostle's original intention. If we select "babes" the meaning is that Paul and his fellow missionaries became childlike with the Thessalonians to identify with them in their beginning stages of Christian growth. That too is a part of gentleness. Paul was able to become all things to all men. "To the weak I became as weak, that I might win the weak. I have become all things to all men, that I might by all means save some" (1 Cor. 9:22). He has reminded us that however far we grow in the Christian faith we must never forget how we got started so that we can tenderly help others begin.

The "gentle" alternative translation is equally demanding. Using a different word in Galatians 5:22, Paul identifies gentleness as a fruit of the Spirit, one of the implanted characteristics of Jesus which is ours as a result of His character transplant in us.[1] The point is that we are empowered by Christ to be as gentle with others as He has been with us. The word implies patience, empathy, merciful compassion and understanding. Paul had been all of these to the new Christians in Thessalonica.

We are left to wonder about how many people in our lives feel either our willingness to enter into their stage of growth or feel gentleness from us. I think of the people who discipled me as Christ began His character transformation in me. It's almost humorous to look back at the person I was. The eccentricities were not easy for people to tolerate. But a band of gentle people nursed me into growth in the new life. I praise God that they never gave up on me. The memory has made me much more tolerant with beginners. In a way we are all constantly beginners. We are never finished growing. Love means listening to people long enough so that we can enter into their lives enthusiastically at whatever stage of growth in Christ they are experiencing. There's always a next step for all of us and we need encouragers who press us to move on.

That's the other part of genuine love Paul delineates in verse 11. His love was also like a father exhorting, encouraging and imploring his children. Babies are lovely but to remain infantile all of our lives would be tragic. So too in the spiritual realm. Paul nursed the Thessalonians as babes in Christ, but he did not leave them there. Christ loves us just as we are but will never allow us to remain satisfied with what we are. Genuine love instigates growth.

Paul uses three words to describe the quality of enabling love we too are to communicate with fatherly concern for people's development. The three participles, exhorting, encouraging and imploring, dramatize the implementation of creative love for another person. The word "exhorting," *parakalountes*, means a strong appeal, to entreat. It implies that we are to help people envision the person Christ wants them to be. But people can picture their full potential only if we give them an example of what adventuresome living in Christ is like. We are to be with people in such a way that they can exclaim, "Now that's what it means to be a mature person in Christ!" There are so few exciting models. The script we give people is usually reserved, timid and mediocre.

I heard a woman express just the opposite. "I have decided to become the kind of person I long for our whole congregation to become so that our church can be an example of what I pray every church in America will be." She has come to grips with the power of her influence. We are all reproducing people in our brand of Christianity. The ministry of exhortation is both verbal and exemplary. We are called to talk to people about what it means to live an exciting, mature life in Christ and give them a picture from our lives of what that could mean for them.

The dynamic decade we've been talking about for the church will require a deep level of maturity from church members. Our society longs to see that Christianity can work. Some fatherly toughness must be coupled with our gentleness to precipitate growth among comfortable church members. Dynamic churches demand and receive growth in discipleship from their members.

But that growth will take place only if exhortation is blended with the second participle: encouraging. Once the goal of maturity is clarified, people need personal help and inspiration to define and take the next steps. The word *paramuthoomenoi* is the enabling, encouraging side of exhortation. Love is catching the pulse beat of people's stage of growth and helping them to move beyond the satisfaction of where they are. But that presupposes that we have earned the right through faithful friendship to make suggestions which can be heard and appropriated. Genuine love over a period of time alone gives us credentials to make suggestions. People must know we are for them and will not reject them because of what they do or say. As Walter Winchell used to say, "In crises, enemies walk out and friends walk in."

The secret of helping people is in the third word of fatherly love. The word is *marturomenoi* meaning "witness" or "testimony." How else can we communicate the adventure of maturing than by sharing with people how Christ has enabled us to grow in the delights and difficulties of life. When we share how He has helped us, vulnerability and viability are communicated. We are not aloof, critical judges always on someone's back to change, but fellow strugglers who also stumble, fall and are picked up by the Master. Often the best way to help a growing Christian move on is to share what we have discovered and learned from our most recent experience of Christ teaching us in the crucible of living.

A true friend's love helps us to learn from what we are passing through in either joy or pain. "What are you learning from what's happening to you?" is a helpful question which frees people to utilize the lessons Christ is teaching. That should be combined with "I know what you mean—I certainly would not be where I am if the Lord had not used my tragedies and triumphs. For example..."

The gentleness of a mother nursing her child combined with the firmness of a father are qualities which Christ develops in both men and women. All of us probably have more of one characteristic than the other. They are not limited to our sex. Both are a part of Christ's love in us.

Now press on to the next aspect of authentic love in Paul's explanation of his relationships with the Thessalonians. *It was also congruent.* His love was outstretched with two arms, offering the gospel with one and his own life with the other. This puts an exclamation point on all that I've tried to communicate thus far in this chapter. "So, affectionately longing for you, we were well-pleased to impart to you not only the gospel of God, but also our own lives, because you have become dear to us" (1 Thess. 2:8). Preaching and living were congruent. Words and action were wed into one. What Paul explained, he exemplified. Congruent love is one of the greatest needs in the contemporary church fellowship and our witness to the world.

Paul worked at his tent-making trade so that he would never be a financial burden on the church. "For you remember, brethren, our labor and toil; for laboring night and day so as not to be a burden to any of you, we preached to you the gospel of God." (v. 9). What a vivid witness that must have been to the Thessalonians!

We can't help but admire the freedom Paul had. So often today's clergy become so dependent on their positions and salaries that their ministry is curtailed. The only way I have ever been able to deal with Paul's challenging example is to be thankful for the privilege of being able to give my full time to being a pastor. And yet, I am ready at any point to do something else for my livelihood if that would help the parish move forward. I never want to fall into the trap of using my ministry to minister to me.

But also there's a further implication here for all of us about congruent love. Often people can't hear what we say because of what we are in our daily lives. Our behavior and attitudes negate our pious language. When we do what love dictates we will be heard in what love articulates.

The test for our inventory of our capacity to love is the extent to which we give ourselves away to people we say we love. That means the surrender to the Master of our time, schedules, priorities, money and resources. Then we need to pray for His guidance of the particular people He's placed on our personal agenda to be His love incarnate. We can't reach everyone. I experience the frustration of the immensity of human need and my limited humanity. There are not enough hours in the day to get to everyone who needs Christ's love through me. Know the feeling? The only solution is to commit each day and relate unreservedly to the people the Lord brings into our lives. He will honor our willingness to develop in-depth, caring relationships. His indwelling Spirit will give us discernment of how most creatively to give ourselves away in each relationship.

A calling of caring is given to every Christian. The new church which is being born in this decade is being built on the ministry of the laity. No congregation can afford enough clergy to care for a congregation. The only hope of the church is for congregations to become caring centers where people love and support each other. Often this happens when a congregation is broken down into small prayer-share-and-care groups that meet consistently during the week. Not only do people learn to support one another in the adventure of

Christian living, but they become alerted to the potential power of their influence to reach more believers at work and in the community. Just think what would happen to our membership rolls if each church member singled out one person, communicated Christ's love, gave himself away lavishly, introduced the person to the new life and led him or her into church membership!

The last thing Paul teaches about *authentic love is that it must be current.* The remainder of chapter 2, from verses 13 to 19, is filled with fresh, up-to-date love. Paul *constantly* thanked God for the Thessalonians and his letter was a stirring reminder to them that he loved them even more than he had when he was with them. Note that his expressions of love are given in the context of the current troubles and afflictions the Thessalonians were facing.

Current love keeps in contact. If we can assume that the Lord will guide us about whom He has placed on our agendas, then it is our responsibility to know what's happening in their lives. I find it helpful to make up a prayer list of the particular people the Lord has singled out for my special concern. Follow-up becomes a necessity. Letters, phone calls, visits, recreational time together, leisurely meals and spontaneous get-togethers keep me current. People ask me, "How can you do that with all you have to do?" My answer is, "If I am too busy to care profoundly for the people God has put on my personal agenda at this time, then I am too busy." I believe the same is true for you. Every Christian must keep time for that special group of Christ-appointed people on his or her prayer list.

When we keep current with people, we know how to say and act out our love. Paul's love sent Timothy back to Thessalonica to find out what was happening to his loved ones in Christ. Imagine what his letter would have been without the data that Timothy reported to him. Feel what it would have been like to talk about how much he loved them without ever mentioning the crises through which they were living.

Keep love current. If we have experienced the other dimensions of authentic love we have dealt with in this chapter, we can love regardless of what people are, do or say. Paul knew about the problems in Thessalonica. He understood what some of the problem-people were doing to weaken and disrupt the fellowship. His letter was on target. Love had freed him to listen. Because he was current he could be incisive.

People need to know that we love them. Picture the church gathered in Thessalonica to hear the reading of Paul's affirming words of love. Dockhands, laborers, business leaders, converted prostitutes from the temples, the rich and the poor, educated and uncultured, Gentiles and completed Jews—all God's people and all needing to know that Paul loved them, knew their struggles and really cared. In that context look at the final verses of the chapter. "For what is our hope, or joy, or crown of rejoicing? Is it not even you in the presence of our Lord Jesus Christ at His coming? For you are our glory and joy" (vv. 19, 20). Feel what this must have meant to them. We dare not take anyone for granted. Everyone needs fresh expressions of love and empathy. Say it!

Life is short. Who are the people in your life today who need to hear words of love rooted in current understanding of what is happening to and around them? The only way to keep our relationship with the Lord vital is to grasp the opportunities to express affirming love to others. Our prayers will soon become empty and shallow if we resist the impetus of His Spirit to love.

Now return to the central image of the scales with which we began the discussion of authentic love. Put your loving on the scale. Does it balance with the Lord's love? In which of the aspects of authentic love do you need to grow? I know mine. And the joy of my tomorrow will be dependent upon what I do about it today.

4

Don't Check Out!

First Thessalonians 3

Stand fast in the Lord.

It was one of those "what's-the-use-why-stay-in-the-battle" kind of days. I was one of the speakers at a conference on church renewal at a small hotel in the mountains. The church leaders from various denominations seemed to be committed to church business as usual. Resistance to change permeated the atmosphere. The gray grimness of defensive institutional religion was written on people's joyless faces. Any efforts to infuse enthusiasm and capture an exciting vision were accepted with pleasant resistance. The woe of the status quo was shouted from the body language of the group.

"Why am I here?" I asked myself. I longed for the charade to end so I could go home to my "let's-go-pull-out-all-the-stops" congregation.

Halfway through the conference I left the meetings to take a walk. As I passed through the lobby of the hotel, I was startled to hear my name spoken by the telephone operator at the switchboard behind the registration counter.

"I'm sorry," she said, "Dr. Ogilvie has checked out." I went over to her to tell her that, indeed, I had not checked out and that I had two more days reserved with the hotel. "There must be some mistake, sir," the befuddled woman said. "According to our records, you've already checked out." There was a mix-up with both registration and housekeeping. The error was corrected and I went on to my walk.

As I strolled along a mountain path, it suddenly hit me. The telephone operator's statement was more prophetic than she had realized. I had checked out! Not from the hotel, but from the conference. I knew that a breakthrough to real communication would require the pain of encounter and possible conflict. Exposing false gods of religious people is a strenuous responsibility. Did I want to go through it again? How much did I really care about these frightened churchmen? Then it dawned on me. I had the same need they had. We all needed courage. I needed a fresh infusion to confront the core of the need in my new friends at the conference and they needed it to go back to their churches to lead a profound renaissance. In a way we all had checked out!

Are you ever tempted to check out from life's battles and tensions? We all have times when we wonder if it's worth the strain. Often we check out from discipleship when the cost of caring becomes exorbitantly high. Or we check out on difficult people or demanding situations. We are still with them but have checked out mentally, emotionally or spiritually. The temptation to give up while we are still in the battle is constantly before us.

The thing I realized on my walk that afternoon is that we all live on the edge of equivocation and need courage. When I got in touch with my feelings, I realized that there was a next step in my pilgrimage that I needed and had been reluctant to take. The sure sign that we are in an authentic relationship with Christ is that there is a bold stride we need to take in being faithful and obedient. He is constantly pressing us on to new adventure where only His courage can sustain us. The more honest I became about where I needed courage, the more sensitive and empathetic I became during the rest of that conference. The Lord helped me open up with the people about my own fears and need for courage. I checked back in. You guessed it—there was a vital breakthrough and by the end of the time together the Lord blessed us all with a fresh touch of His power.

Paul was deeply concerned about the danger of the Thessalonians checking out on faithful discipleship. He couldn't get them off his mind and heart. His worry over them prompted him to send Timothy back to find out how they were doing. The report Timothy brought back to the apostle in Corinth was mixed. Yes, their authentic conversion had taken deep roots, and yes, they were holding fast in spite of persecution. But some were wavering, and all needed courage. So Paul's word to them was to "stand fast in the Lord" (1 Thess. 3:8). This is the jugular verse.

And Paul needed to stand fast in Corinth. Things were not any easier for him there than they were for the new Christians in Thessalonica. Two realities converged to fire the apostle to write stirring words of courage to his beloved friends. One was his knowledge of their need and the other was the Lord's gift to him in his needs. The Lord always gives us what we need, not only for ourselves, but for others who are confronting similar needs.

I am very thankful for the book of Acts as a companion to a study of Paul's Epistles. It helps us identify what he was going through during the time he wrote many of his letters of love and encouragement. This is especially true of the Thessalonian Epistles. In Acts 18 we discover what was happening to Paul when he received word of the Thessalonians and wrote this first letter. The courage he admonished them to have, had been given to him in an abundant measure for his own conflicts and temptation to retreat.

The difficulties in Macedonia and then the rejection in Athens left the apostle ill-prepared for new opposition in

Corinth. The Jews not only opposed him but blasphemed him (see Acts 18:6). We are sure he questioned why he should persist in preaching the gospel with love. Then one night the Lord came to him. His words were filled with courage-infusing strength. "Do not be afraid, but speak, and do not keep silent; for I am with you, and no one will attack you to hurt you; for I have many people in this city" (Acts 18:9, 10). The message was undeniably clear: Stop being afraid; don't become silent; I am with you. Take courage! The gathering storm of conflict had created panic in the battle-weary Paul. He knew only too well what it could do to him and his mission. Every person who dares to face reality knows moments and moods like that—the temptation to check out on our duty. The Lord matched an encroaching cowardice with enabling courage.

Now, I believe that this midnight encounter with the Lord occurred about the same time Timothy returned with news of the Thessalonians. Paul's advice to them in this third chapter was molded out of the raw material of his own discoveries of authentic prayer as the source of authentic courage.

Allow me to return to our working definition of *authentic* once again. Authentic prayer is of undisputable origin, genuine, congruent and current. The source is in the Lord Himself. Prayer begins with Him. He comes to us so that we can come to Him. He initiates the desire to listen to Him so that what we ask is in keeping with what He is more ready to give than we may be to ask. It is genuine in that it is an honest dealing with reality and not wish-dreams. Powerful praying occurs when we allow the Lord to talk to us about our real needs so that we can talk to Him about our perplexities in the light of His perspective. So often we pray about trivialities when our hearts are bursting with pain. Real communication occurs in prayer when we deal with the gut issues which are pulling us apart. There is congruity between what we pray and the need that is really facing us.

Prayer is conversation with the Lord. A dialogue which is 75 percent listening and 25 percent speaking. It's like unloading to a dear friend. People who have no secrets from each other never lack for subjects of conversation; they do not weigh their words. There is nothing held back. Thomas Chalmers was right when he said that prayer does not just enable us to do a greater work for God. Prayer is a greater work for God. Prayer and courage are inseparable. Paul wrote this portion of his encouragement to the Thessalonians out of the rich resources of the courage the Lord had given him in prayer.

Chapter 3 is a classic statement of the meaning of intercessory prayer. It describes the identification and intensity of mutuality which makes prayer for others a source of courage in their lives. Note how Paul tells the Thessalonians that he knows what they are going through. He identified with their tribulation (see v. 4), shared his own affliction and distress (see v. 7), and then went on to say that he was "praying exceedingly" (v. 10). The double compound adverb for "exceedingly" in Greek is *huperekperissou*, meaning abundantly, overflowing all bounds. Paul prayed without ceasing for his loved ones in Thessalonica. Night and day!

Don't give up! That was Paul's message to the young Christians and now to us. What the Lord had said to him, he said to the Thessalonians. It becomes the Lord's personal word to us today. We all need courage and need to pray exceedingly for courage for one another. The prolonged study of this intensely personal portion of Paul's letter has prompted me to write three things about courage and how we find it in life's tight places when we are tempted to check out on life.

First of all, *courage is fear which has said its prayers.* Paul and the Thessalonians had fear in common. And so do we. If we are not attempting something which creates the human reaction of fear we are probably not living life as it was meant to be lived. Fear in the soul-stretching challenges drives us to prayer. Eddie Rickenbacker knew what he was talking about when he said that courage is doing what you're afraid to do. There is no courage unless you're scared and are driven to your knees. Thomas Fuller, English divine and author (1608-1661), said, "Fear can keep a man out of danger, but courage can support him in it." The psalmist discovered the Lord's antidote to fear when he heard Him say in the depth of his soul, "Call upon me in the day of trouble: I will deliver thee, and thou shalt glorify me" (Ps. 50:15, *KJV*). Like all of us, he wanted to escape life's challenges. "Oh that I had wings like a dove! for then would I fly away, and be at rest" (Ps. 55:6, *KJV*). But honest praying had not allowed such a flight from reality and responsibility. Prayer is not an escape but an encounter. Nehemiah discovered that when his frightened friends encouraged him to check out from the endless conflict and discouragement of rebuilding the walls of Jerusalem. His response should be a memorized motto for us: "Should a man like me flee? And could one such as I go into the temple to save his life?" (Neh. 6:11). Carlyle said that life begins with the quiet estimate of ourselves that will not let us play the coward. And that quiet estimate of our fear and the Lord's power is the essence of authentic prayer.

Second, *courage is the Lord's special gift for the challenge of answered prayer.* We hear so much about the pain of unanswered prayer. What about answered prayer? When the Lord shows us in a clear and unmistakable way what we must do, that's when we need courage. Our future relationship with the Lord hangs in the balance when we receive our marching orders. Often we would rather muddle in indecision. Most of us know more than we have acted on. Our problem is not unanswered but answered prayer. When we know what we must do to love a person unconditionally in spite of our judgments, when we discern what righteousness demands in a complicated situation, when we clearly understand the Lord's guidance for costly discipleship—that's when courage is given.

Remember the timing of the Lord when the people of Israel had to cross the Jordan and go into the Promised Land? He told Joshua that when the priests carrying the ark put their feet in the water, He would roll back the Jordan so they could pass through. Experience that from within the skin of one of those priests! The first step into the water must have been difficult. But when the soles of their feet were wet, the Lord opened the way through the riverbed. Joshua and those priests anguished over the pain of answered prayer. And so do we. It is when the soles of our feet are wet with the first step of obedience that courage is given and the way opens for us.

Next, *authentic courage is something we take because the Lord has taken hold of us.* Courage is an offered gift which we must take. The psalmist discovered that. The Lord said to him, "Be strong, and let your heart *take courage"* (Ps. 31:24, italics added). Courage is ours for the taking. It must be claimed and appropriated. This is the salient thrust of Jesus' offer to His disciples on the night before the crucifixion. I like the accurate rendering of the Greek in the *New American Standard Bible.* "These things I have spoken to you, that in *Me* you may have peace. In the world you have tribulation, but *take* courage; I have overcome the world" (John 16:33, italics added). This translation is stronger than others which say, "Be of good cheer." The word is *tharseite* in Greek, active imperative. It comes from *tharsos,* courage. The imperative carries the challenge to "take courage." We can take it only because the Lord has taken us. He has a tight grip on us.

Think of the crucial times this offer is made in the New Testament. It was spoken to the paralytic in Matthew 9:2 when the Lord said, "Take courage . . . your sins are forgiven." The same assurance was spoken to the woman who pressed through the crowd and touched the Master. "Take courage, your faith has made you well" (Matt. 9:22). The people around blind Bartimaeus said it when Jesus responded to his plea. "Take courage, . . . He is calling you" (Mark 10:49).

In prayer, the Lord takes hold of us with one hand and offers courage with the other. Horatius Bonar experienced this and penned a triumphant assurance.

> *Thy love to me, O God,*
> *Not mine, O Lord to Thee,*
> *Can rid me of this dark unrest*
> *And set my spirit free.*
> *Let me no more my comfort draw*
> *From my frail hold on Thee.*
> *Rather in this rejoice with awe*
> *Thy mighty grasp on me.*[2]

Dr. Alexander Whyte, that great preacher of another generation at St. George's West Church in Edinburgh once asked a friend, "How are you keeping?" The answer was profound. "Doctor, I'm not keeping; I'm being kept." Paul would have agreed. He used the Greek word for guard when he assured the Philippians of the peace of God. The word is often translated as "keep" in the modern translations. I am delighted that the *New King James Bible* renders it as "guard" in Philippians 4:7 "And the peace of God, which surpasses all understanding, will guard your hearts and minds through Christ Jesus."

Peace in the midst of conflict is the evidence of the Lord's indwelling power. Paul prayed that the Thessalonians would experience courage to face their extremities, grow in love, and grasp the opportunities around them. He longed for the Lord to establish their "hearts blameless in holiness" (1 Thess. 3:13). The word *establish* is from a Greek infinitive of purpose. It means support. The Lord will support us in the things He guides. We will never be alone. All we need to do is pray for that support for ourselves and others.

The last thing I want to say about courage is that *courage* is the power to overcome rather than overreact to circumstances. Jesus told the disciples to take courage because He had overcome the world. Amazing! He spoke that before He went to the anguish of Calvary. He knew God would see Him through, bringing the best out of the worst.

The Greek word used to translate the Master's Aramaic word for "overcome" is *nikaō*, to be victorious, to conquer. It is in the perfect active, meaning that which is done but continues. The same word is used repeatedly by John in his epistles. "This is the victory that has overcome the world" (1 John 5:4). The word for "victory" and "overcome" are two different forms of the same root, *nikaō:* the victory, *nikē;* which overcomes, *nikēsasa.* The tense indicates a single victory. It implies the victory of Christ over Satan, sin, and death. That victory is the fulcrum for our present assurance of victory in our battles today.

> *The heart that prays soars high*
> *   on strong glad wings,*
> *And finds repose beyond earth's rending things,*
> *It hears above the turmoil and the strife*
> *The ceaseless, matchless melody of life...*
> *The heart that prays envisions tasks divine,*
> *And yields itself to fashion love's design.*[3]

Note that John goes on, "Who is he who overcomes the world, but he who believes that Jesus is the Son of God?" (v. 5). The single victory of Christ has constantly recurring application. The present active indicative means we receive residuals every day as we claim what Christ has accomplished as the basis of our courage in each new problem. We can be sure of this: there is a victory of the Lord in every impossible complexity!

James sounded the same trumpet. "My brethren, count it all joy when you fall into various trials, knowing that the testing of your faith produces patience. But let patience have its perfect work, that you may be perfect and complete, lacking nothing" (Jas. 1:2-4).

Joy in trials? How can that be? Joy in times of success, prosperity and accomplishment, but joy in trials—that seems contrary to our experience. Yet this is James's word: we are to be joyous in trials.

The truth is that joy is the unassailable, undisturbable, undeniable experience of those who know Christ in the midst of difficulty. Happiness is always dependent on our circumstances—the root of the word gives it away, it means chance. Joy is way beyond that; it is the outward expression of the inner experience of God's grace in each new vortex of difficulty.

Note the magnificent progression in James's thought. Trials test our faith; this test produces steadfastness and steadfastness develops us toward our goal. Start from the end and work backward and you can see what James is talking about. To be "perfect and complete" is the purpose of God in our lives. This means that we accomplish our reason for being: to glorify God and enjoy Him forever. But we get to that point only as the difficulties of life throw us back in absolute dependence on our Lord. As we trust Him, we learn that He is utterly reliable. Our faith grows and becomes steadfast, rock-like. Think of Psalm 118: "His steadfast love endures for ever" (*RSV*) His steadfast love produces a steadfast endurance. We are not pushed around by life. It is no longer what life does to us but what we do in life; not what happens to us, but what we cause to happen because of our faith.

That is where joy begins and grows. The more we experience grace in our troubles, the more joyous we will be in those things which defeat people who do not know grace. Then we can pray, "Lord Jesus, all we need to know today is that you are with us in our trials. That will give us the courage we need; that will put steel in our backbones. Use the very things we go through to develop us toward the purpose you have for us. Thank you for the difficult things which will be the opportunity for new joy today."

The motto of the newspaperman, Joseph Pulitzer, owed much to Jesus: "Comfort the afflicted and afflict the comfortable." Jesus does just that! He comforts those who mourn over their own, others', and the world's suffering. The Greek word for comfort means "to call to the side of." Christ stands by our side when we become sensitive to the needs of our world and our part in it. When we become comfortable in any other security than Him, He unsettles us with His disturbing exposure of what life was meant to be.

Only Christ knows when we need to be comforted and when we need to be afflicted. He knows when to assure and when to alarm. Our own judgment of our needs is often wrong. When we think we need comforting, He often comes with a disturbing challenge which gets us on our feet. Then, too, when we do not know our need for fortification, He builds us up in love to face some imminent difficulty we must go through.

The wonderful good news is that He stands beside us. The Messiah was called the Comforter. Jesus promised to return in the power of the Holy Spirit, the Comforter. He comforts us by helping us to get a perspective on what we face, to see what He is teaching us in it, to learn what He can do with a life surrendered to Him and to experience the power of His sustaining Spirit. The comfort of Christ is the unlimited source of our courage.

Paul really believed in the power of his intercessory prayers for the comforting of the Thessalonians and their prayers for him. Throughout his letters to them he repeatedly reminded them that he was praying for them and that he needed their prayers for him. This was based on the deep conviction that God delights to answer the prayers of His people for one another. As our Father, He longs for us to know the love expressed in intercessory prayer for brothers and sisters in His eternal family.

Dora Greenwell asks and answers the crucial question about intercessory prayer for courage in others. "We know that God's nature is unchangeable; are we sure that His will is equally so? Is the wish, the submitted wish of a human heart, able to alter the counsel of the Almighty? Can the humble request of believing lips restrain, accelerate, change the settled order of events? Can prayer make things that are not, be as though they were? Yes, a thousand times yes! Intercession is the mother tongue of the whole family of Christ."[4]

We are part of the priesthood of all believers. We have been given great authority to go to God on behalf of others. A prayer for courage in another person's life will be heard and answered. We have been given the keys of the kingdom and intercessory prayer is one of the most strategic of those keys. What we loose through prayer in Jesus' name will be loosed in heaven.

I don't know about you, but the example of Paul's love for the Thessalonians and his intercessory prayer for them has prompted me to evaluate my priorities. How much time do I give to being a priest in prayers for others? How about you? As for me, this calling must now have a much higher priority. The courage of so many depends on it.

There is a powerful story told of Leonardo da Vinci. One day in his studio he started work on a large canvas. He labored on it, choosing the subject carefully, arranging the perspective, sketching the outline, applying the colors and developing the background. Then, for some unknown reason, he stopped with the painting still unfinished. He called one of his students and asked him to finish. The student was flabbergasted. How could he finish a painting by one of the world's truly great masters? He protested his inadequacy and insufficiency for so challenging a task. But the great artist silenced him, "Will not what I have done inspire you to do your best?" he asked.

That is really Jesus' question, isn't it? He began it all

2,000 years ago. His life, message, death, resurrection and living presence started the great painting of the redemption of the world. He has given us the task to finish the painting. But there is a difference. Da Vinci left his student alone; Jesus never does that. He has given us the color palette, and whispers His guiding insight to us at each uncertain stroke. We cannot shrink from the task. The challenge and inspiration press us on.

We sometimes get bogged down in the daily routine of living and forget the essential task of our life. We are part of a new breed of humanity. The church is to be a new kind of society of love and forgiveness. Our task is nothing less than the changing and transformation of the world, beginning with ourselves, our families and our sphere of influence. In Christ we are given our image of true living. We are to know the same power and peace manifested in His life. What He has done and who He is inspires us to get on with the painting today with the Master's touch close at hand.

Don't check out! Pray and take courage.

5

Distinctly Different

First Thessalonians 4:1-12

For this is the will of God, your sanctification.

"For God's sake grow up!" These sharp words of challenge were given to a man whose faith had not penetrated into his character and relationships. His commitment to Christ had remained a sentimental, infantile evasion and equivocation. He was not childlike, but childish. All of his attitudes and values were the same as he had before accepting Christ. Immobilized on dead center, he resisted growth at every turn. The troublesome flaws in his character remained unhealed. He needed to grow up—in Christ.

A commitment to Christ as Saviour *and* Lord is a commitment to grow. The Lord is never finished with us. The more we discover of ourselves, the more we have to give to Christ's control. The more we discover of Christ, the deeper we grow in our relationship with Him. Every day demands honest facing of ourselves and areas in which we need His transformation. Prayer, Bible study, sensitivity to the Lord's presence and penetrating reformation—all result in the realization of the need for further growth. We have been called to be distinctly different!

The other day I was shocked to realize a need to grow in an area of my own life. Without knowing it, I had fallen into a manipulative pattern of grandstanding benevolence with my family. I had arranged some very fine opportunities of travel and announced them in a way that demanded approbation. What insecurity had prompted that? My wife alerted me, in as kind a way as she could, to how I was coming across. Suddenly, I was aware of an old pattern of relating to people I love. A prolonged time with my Lord exposed the trouble. For some reason an old insecurity had reared its ugly head. I had done the right thing for the wrong reason. Rather than doing the right thing out of love, I had done it to assure the flow of affirmation.

The interesting thing about this unsettling realization of the need to grow was that it had been preceded by a period of delicious satisfaction over my growth in Christ. I was thankful for all that the Lord was doing in my life and delighted by the progress we were making together. And then this disturbing realization of a new need to grow. Once again I experienced a truth I know, but often forget: the Lord is the potter and I am the clay; He has begun to mold me into His own image and He will be refashioning me all through my life. Every period of gratitude over what He's accomplished with me will be followed by an exposure of a new need to grow.

We all bring an old nature into the Christian life. The new creation in Christ is both immediate and gradual. When we surrender our lives to Christ, accepting Him as our Saviour and Lord, we are ushered into a dynamic relationship. The moment we say yes! to Him we are assured of eternal life, His presence, *and* a never ending growth in His likeness. Our eternal destiny is no longer in question but our character is always in process. The Christian life is a never-ending growth in depth.

The reason for this is that becoming a new creation in

Christ is a thorough, ongoing character reorientation. We have been conditioned by the religious, cultural, and social values of our time. Attitudes, reactions, goals and thought patterns have been inadvertently ingrained into the fiber of our natures. When we become Christians everything is suddenly exposed to Christ's scrutinizing renovation. Life as we have lived it is consistently exposed to a startling comparison with life as the Lord meant it to be. We can appreciate what's happening to us by observation of what the Lord longs to do in the lives of others.

Think of how disturbed we are by the behavior of some Christians. We become indignant when a person who professes to be "in Christ" does or says something which boldly contradicts his or her faith. Then after our flush of righteous indignation, finger-pointing, and lip-smacking judgmentalism, the Lord turns His searchlight of truth and honesty on us. "What about the contradictions in your own life? What if people knew about your inner thoughts, fantasies, distortions and selfish attitudes?" Suddenly our judgments are replaced by empathy. Given the same temptations or pressures, we may not have been any better. We are all unfinished and need to pray as well as sing, "Finish then Thy new creation, pure, unselfish let us be."

Focus the areas where you need to grow in the new life in Christ. If He were to diagnose your next steps, what would He prescribe? Recently in a Covenant Bible Study group in which my wife and I are participants, each of us was challenged to write out a prescription he or she felt the Lord would write. It was enlightening to hear what each wrote. Though many in the group are seasoned saints who have lived the Christian life for years, all of us knew that we had barely begun. The Lord is up to a magnificent thing in all of us. We all needed affirmation of the progress He had made with us and a clear delineation of the next steps in being distinctly different people. Our need to grow up in Christ is not unlike that of the Thessalonians.

In the fourth chapter of Paul's letter, he turns from thankful affirmation to urgent exhortation. The key word of the first 12 verses of this chapter is *sanctification.* The jugular verse is 3: "For this is the will of God, your sanctification." The Greek word for sanctification is *hagiasmos.* It has its root in *hagios,* "holy," and is a kindred term to holiness. The word holy, when applied to persons, means belonging to God, set apart, destined to live for His glory. When we are chosen and called by Him, we become holy, not because we are perfect, but because we now belong to the Lord. Sanctification is the process of growing in holiness.

Our search for a deeper understanding of sanctification ushers us into a survey of the Scriptures. The assurance of holiness was first clearly articulated to Israel through Moses by God on Sinai: "Now then, if you will indeed obey My voice and keep My covenant, then you shall be My own possession among all the peoples, for all the earth is Mine; and you shall be to Me a kingdom of priests and a holy nation" (Exod. 19:5,6). The word for "possession" in Hebrew is *treasure.* Israel was the treasured possession of Yahweh.

This same triumphant affirmation was sounded by Moses when he asserted the specialness of God's people. "For you are a holy people to the Lord your God; the Lord your God has chosen you to be a people for His own possession [special treasure again] out of all the peoples who are on the face of the earth. The Lord did not set His love on you nor choose you because you were more in number than any of the peoples, for you were the fewest of all peoples, but because the Lord loved you and kept the oath which He swore to your forefathers, the Lord brought you out by a mighty hand, and redeemed you from the house of slavery, from the hand of Pharaoh king of Egypt. Know therefore that the Lord your God, He is God, the faithful God, who keeps His covenant and His lovingkindness to a thousandth generation with those who love Him and keep His commandments" (Deut. 7:6-9).

In Leviticus 19:2 the source and substance of our sanctification is clearly stated. "You shall be holy, for I the Lord your God am holy." Our holiness comes from the Lord who has appointed us to be His people and share his nature.

We are recipients of this holy calling through the new covenant in Christ. The new Israel, the church, is assured of an even greater election to sanctification. In Romans 12:1 Paul challenges us to present our lives to God, holy and acceptable. He reminds us that our lives are God's temple and that the temple is holy (see 1 Cor. 3:17), calls us to be holy in body and spirit (see 1 Cor. 7:34), affirms us as holy and beloved (see Col. 3:12), and encourages us to be upright, holy, and self-controlled (see Titus 1:8). Peter sums this up with an astounding declaration. "But you are a chosen generation, a royal priesthood, a holy nation, His own special people, that you may proclaim the praises of Him who has called you out of darkness into His marvelous light; who once were not a people but are now the people of God, who had not obtained mercy but now have obtained mercy" (1 Pet. 2:9,10).

Sanctification is the process of becoming distinctly different. It is the miracle of a character transformation in which we become more and more like Christ. We were created for growth toward maturity in every facet of life. We can be more than we ever imagined possible. "Christ in you, the hope of glory" (Col. 1:27) would be a beautiful way of vividly describing the source and substance of sanctification.

In the light of this survey of Scripture about sanctification, we can appreciate more fully what Paul was trying to communicate in these first 12 verses of 1 Thessalonians 4. Verses 1 and 2 lead up to his major thrust in verse 3. The apostle reminds the Thessalonians of what he, Silas, and Timothy explained and exemplified about the new life in Christ. The new converts had learned how to "walk and please God." Now Paul calls them to abound in that more and more. "Don't stop; you've only begun!" he seems to be saying.

He reminds them of the commandments he and his companions gave them through Jesus Christ. The word "commandment" in Greek is the same as a word for a military order. General Paul had passed on the orders of the Commander in Chief! Christ Himself is the author of our sanctification.

Writing with the Lord's authority, Paul spells out several crucial aspects of the sanctification he desires for the counter-culture Christians in Thessalonica. Growth in Christ will occur through a distinctly different quality of life in the home, on the job and in the church. Christianity had brought a radically new concept of all three in the commercial city. The real test of our growth in Christ is in those three areas of life today.

The first, *growth in Christ in the home,* was a new concept to the Thessalonians. Immorality was a way of life in Thessalonica. Women were held in low esteem and the family had little permanence. The pagan temples throughout the city kept a large staff of prostitutes. Worship and fornication went hand in hand. Women were considered things for pleasure. Demosthenes expressed the belief of many: "We keep prostitutes for pleasure; we keep mistresses for the day-to-day needs of the body; we keep wives for the begetting of children and for the faithful guardianship of our home"[5] Most men had several wives throughout a lifetime and extra-marital sex was not only accepted, but expected.

Among the Jews in Thessalonica, divorce was permitted for a multiplicity of absurd reasons. A man could dismiss his wife simply by writing a writ of divorce. The liberal rabbis had a long list of acceptable reasons for divorce, all the way from ruining a husband's meal to raising her voice loud enough to be heard by the neighbors. It was a man's world in which women had no rights and little or no dignity.

This was the kind of "thinging-it" culture in which Paul preached the gospel to both Greeks and Jews. The converts from both groups were called back to God's original intention for sex, marriage and the family. Echoing his Master,

Paul elevated women, admonished sexual purity, taught the sacredness of marriage, and encouraged new reverence for the family. The Christians were to be distinctly different, Christ-guided, holy people. No wonder they ran into hostility and persecution!

Paul not only demanded sexual purity but *absolute honesty on the job,* in business dealings. R.C.H. Lenski in his *Interpretation of St. Paul's Epistles . . . ,* observes that, "The two outstanding vices of paganism were sexual and commercial vileness and greed." And Paul called the Christians to model a totally new quality of integrity. In a world that held laborers and menial work in disdain, the apostle earned his own living as a tentmaker and challenged the Christians to work with their hands industriously. In the marketplace, the Christians were to be distinguished by their reliability and truthfulness in all dealings. How they worked was as crucial as how they said their prayers.

Next, Paul talks about *the inseparable relationship between growth in Christ and growth in brotherly love.* He affirms their progress in being a loving fellowship and then urges them to "increase more and more." Our relationships with fellow believers are a test of our sanctification. The church is a "holy" fellowship. We belong to our Lord and are to be to each other what He has been to us. The more we grow in Christ's love and forgiveness, the more we are able to care for fellow believers.

How often the divisions and discords within the church contradict its message. The world laughs at our inability to live what we preach so eloquently. We bring our culturally conditioned attitudes into the fellowship of the church. Criticism, competition, judgmentalism, gossip are often more prevalent than in a secular club! Paul reminds us that the church is to be the provisional denomination for all to see how He meant His people to lovingly affirm, encourage and enable one another. Sanctification should result in mature relationships. Our old nature, defensive and insecure, always looking out for ourselves and our rights, is to be re-placed by the new nature in Christ. His indwelling power becomes the source of unconditional, unqualified love. We were meant to astound the world by our relationships. Every-one longs to love and be loved. Often the most attractive witness to a nonbeliever is what Christ has done to change our attitudes and ways of relating to others.

I have dealt with these three aspects of Paul's delineation of sanctification not only to be faithful to our exposition of the Scripture, but to show how growth in Christ touches very practical and personal facets of life. Our consideration need not be limited to these examples. Our greatest needs may be the same as those Paul mentions or in others. The essential question, however, is where do you and I need to grow up to the "measure of the stature of the fullness of Christ" (Eph. 4:13)? The transforming process of sanctifica-tion means a total reorientation of our thinking, feelings, attitudes, goals and priorities.

One of my members who recently began our congrega-tion's daily discipline of prayer and Bible study remarked, "I am shocked to discover how many of my basic presupposi-tions are essentially non-biblical. I am an intellectual and yet I'm still in kindergarten as far as knowing and living on the basis of the Bible and the Lord's guidance." He's being sanc-tified!

I wish the same could be said of a Christian leader who carries heavy responsibilities and has a large following. But he uses people. When they have served their purpose, he casts them aside. A concerned person remarked, "There's a terrible chink in his armor, a flaw in his personality. Great regions of his life have never been touched by Christ." Shar-ing this insight with this leader was not easy. It took hours of building confidence before we could talk about it and seek Christ's healing. His skyrocketing career had left out sanc-tification. A breakthrough came when I was able to share how Christ has been enabling constant growth in my life. He is not finished with any of us, especially me. A friendship has grown with this leader in which we share our needs to grow and pray for each other.

A woman who came to me for counseling confessed a problem in her marriage. She had been a Christian for years and yet found relationships painfully difficult. She was insecure, unable to give herself to others, and plagued with low self-esteem. She probably would have remained in her immaturity if a crisis in her marriage had not forced her to discover how to grow up emotionally in Christ.

I've just finished reading the fascinating book, *The Up and Outer*, by a friend and officer in our church, Fred Foster. He describes his release from alcoholism some years ago. His life went bump on bottom below bottom, not on skid row but in the plush offices of the New York advertising world and the expense account luxury of elegant bars and compulsive drinking. He was transformed by a traumatic encounter with Christ. His account of what followed is exciting. As he began to pray, read the Bible, participate in deep-caring fellowship groups, Christ began the long process of reshaping the core of his personality. The years of growth have produced the dynamic man Fred is today.

Another example is an officer of an eastern church who was a negative, uptight rules-and-regulations churchman. He blocked progress at every turn. People began to wonder how he ever got elected to serve on the church board. Fortunately his fellow officers loved him into a realization that his manipulative methods were not working any better at church than they were at home or his office. Gracious acceptance coupled with honest confrontation edged him off the plateau of resistance to growth he was on. I met him at a conference when he was in the midst of his metamorphosis. He was excited about all he was discovering of the new person Christ was liberating him to be.

Each month our church accepts many into membership who have attended our new members classes. Many of them are new converts to Christ. I am gratified by their excitement about Christ and the church. The challenge is to help them know that the joy they are experiencing is only a taste of what the Lord has in store for them. It will not all be smooth and easy. The Lord will continue to penetrate until all of life is under His guidance and power. A young actor who has been a Christian for a year caught the challenge of this. "I'm sure not what I was, nor am I what I will be!" he exclaimed. Not a bad definition of sanctification. The loving Father has His hand on the clay!

I am aware of the unsettling impact of what I have tried to say in this chapter. It may have made you uneasy. Perhaps you have been satisfied with your level of growth. And yet, are you really? I realize that I am asking you and me to be honestly analytical about our life in Christ. In what ways have we grown in this past month? What new discovery about Christ has reoriented our thinking and motivated new behavior? What have we discovered about ourselves that needs to be surrendered to our Lord's refining fire? He's not done with us. Thank Him for that! We are holy people—we belong to Him. We are growing in holiness—being made like Him. And the best is still to come. We are becoming distinctly different people. Now we can say,

> *And every virtue we possess*
> *And every victory won*
> *And every thought of holiness*
> *Are His alone.*[6]

6

Hope in a World Like This

First Thessalonians 4:13—5:11

*But I do not want you to be ignorant, brethren,
concerning those who have fallen asleep, that you
not sorrow as others who have no hope.*

The man at the next table in a restaurant where I was having breakfast punctuated his reading of the morning paper with deep groans of discouragement. Each page of the current national and international news brought a more profound sigh expressing the man's frustration with the world.

A lovely young waitress became concerned as she poured him another cup of coffee. "Is everything alright, sir?" she inquired with alarm. "You seem to be very upset about something."

"You bet I am! Haven't you read the morning paper? I'm sick to death of all the bad news," he replied with consternation.

"You've got to have hope!" the young woman said timidly.

The man's response was a classic. Anger mingled with frustration. The question he asked the waitress is on everyone's heart these days. "Hope? How can you have hope in a world like this?"

How would you have answered this pessimist? I turned to him and picked up on the wording of his question. "I don't have hope in our *world*, but I have *hope* in the world," I said, purposely playing on the words.

"Now what do you mean by that?!" was his anticipated response. I moved over to his table for my second cup of coffee, grasping the serendipity the Lord had arranged.

I tried to explain that the one thing the world could not provide is hope. Hope is illusive: you can never find it by searching for it. It is inadvertent, coming from something else. The world—possibilities, people, progress—are all unreliable sources of hope. They always let us down. The reason for the virulent hopelessness of our time is that it has finally dawned on us that no leader, negotiated peace, armed might, or human cleverness can bring the utopia we've believed was the goal of history. The only way we can live with confidence in any period of history is to have an ultimate conviction about what will happen at the end of history. Where is it all leading? Only a hope that covers all the exigencies of God's plan and purpose for history will sustain us in this turbulent phase of history.

Emil Brunner, Swiss theologian, said, "What oxygen is for the lungs, such is hope for the meaning of life." The spiritual asphyxiation of our time is the result of a profound lack of hope. The false gods of our inadequate hoping have fallen from their thrones. We've lost the idea that everything will eventually work out; that given time, we can solve the soul-sized problems which beset us. And I say: Thank God! The disillusionment of our times is the raw material of a new receptivity in all of us in which authentic hope can be born.

Authentic hope must have an ultimately reliable source, sustain us in all of life's circumstances, and answer all of our questions about present times in the light of the end times. Only Jesus Christ can give that kind of authentic hope. Consistent, lasting hope is a relational dynamic which comes from a personal, intimate trust in the One who came, comes, and is coming. All three dimensions are required for a liberating hope. One without the other, or especially the first two without the last, will leave us unprepared to deal with the questions and quandaries of life today. Some of us are clear about the Christ who came but are uncertain about how He intervenes in our needs today. Others are sure about what He did and does, but are very unsure about what He will do when He returns, not only as Lord of life, but ultimately as Lord of history as we know it. The lack of clear preaching and teaching about the Second Coming and the end times have left us without authentic Christian hope.

When Paul preached the gospel in Thessalonica, he proclaimed the Christ of the threefold advent. He told the faith-engendering story of the incarnation, crucifixion, resurrection and ascension of Jesus Christ. Then he shared the courage-infusing assurance of Christ's presence and power with them. But all of this was climaxed in the fear-dispelling good news that Christ would be coming back in a second advent as victorious Lord of history.

Unlike many of us who are more sure of the Lord who came and comes than we are of the Lord who is coming, the Thessalonians became obsessed with questions and concerns about Christ's return. Paul had preached the Lord's return with such an intimation of imminence that the Thessalonians expected the Second Coming immediately. This caused some of them to forgo responsibilities while waiting for the glorious event. When Timothy and Silas visited them on behalf of the apostle, they sensed the need for enlightenment on this crucial matter. They reported the problem to Paul. I am thankful for the confusion in Thessalonica for it occasioned a clear word from the Lord through Paul in what he wrote them. He claimed that the Lord had spoken directly to him about the matter. "For this we say to you by the word of the Lord" (1 Thess. 4:15). Direct revelation is implied.

What Paul wrote to his friends is now one of the most salient passages in the New Testament about the progression of the Second Coming. Coupled with an in-depth study of Jesus' own words in Matthew 24 and Mark 13, plus Revelation 20, we discover a hope that is founded on the firm foundation of what the return of Christ, the end of history, and His ultimate triumph will be. We will now consider 1 Thessalonians 4:13 through 5:11 as Paul's answer to the questions being raised by the Thessalonians, but also as the biblical delineation of the phases of Christ's return.

There was grave concern among the Thessalonian Christians about those who had died. The term "fallen asleep" means death in verse 13. Would they miss the Lord's return? These questions reveal how imminently they had expected the Lord. Paul's incisive word to them is filled with hope for our anxiety about death. "But I do not want you to be ignorant, brethren, concerning those who have fallen asleep, that you not sorrow as others who have no hope." Death is not an ending for a Christian, but only a transition in eternal life.

All of our fears are rooted into our fear of death. We cannot live *authentically* until we have faced the fact of our physical demise and are convinced of the eternal destiny of our souls. "If in this life only we have hope in Christ, we are of all men the most pitiable" (1 Cor. 15:19). The new life in Christ assures us that when we die we will walk through the valley of the shadow of death with Him and will dwell with Him in glory forever. As George MacDonald, Scottish novelist and poet (1824-1905), put it, "I came from God, and I'm going back to God, and I won't have any gaps of death in the middle of my life."

Christ defeated death once for all, and those of us who have accepted Him as Lord and Saviour need fear it no longer. Verse 14 in 1 Thessalonians 4 drives home the assurance. "For if we believe that Jesus died and rose again, so also God will bring with Him those who sleep in Jesus." The preposition "in" really means "through or by means of Jesus" in the Greek. Therefore, the most accurate rendering would be "those who died through Jesus," meaning those who died in confident trust in, and were raised up by, Jesus. Here is a description of heaven as life with the Lord for eternity. Life as it was meant to be cannot be crammed into this brief span of physical life. "Whether we wake or sleep, we should live together with Him," Paul asserts in 5:10, indicating that whether we are physically alive or spiritually alive after death, we are in union with the Lord.

This assurance is crucial for what Paul goes on to say. The language is poetic and pictorial, but keep in mind the established conviction of the apostle that those who have died are with the Lord.

Now Paul moves on to describe what has been called the rapture. When the Lord returns He "will descend from heaven with a shout, with the voice of an archangel, and with the trumpet of God" (4:16). Those who have died will share in the triumphant event.

Allow your mind to linger on that momentous event. Picture Christ, the company of heaven, loved ones who have gone on to heaven, all participating in the victorious intervention. Christians here on earth will be called to join them and together we will all share in worshiping. What will it be like? Human rhetoric is inadequate to describe it. All we know is that when we are liberated from the limitations of this life, we will be able to know Christ as He is and we will be known as we are. We will give Him unfettered praise and adoration and we will enjoy unencumbered fellowship of the saints with Christ. What more do we need to know? The Christ who came, comes daily, is coming. Are we ready, expectant?

Many who read this passage about the rapture become confused about what seems to be an assumption that the Christians in their graves would rise from the grave to be a part of the glorious event. What does Paul mean by the wording of the last sentence in verse 16? It needs Spirit-guided reflection. "And the dead in Christ will rise first." Does the apostle mean that those who have died are still in their graves? Or did he mean to imply that there was some kind of interim state for those who died until the Second Coming? Hardly. My understanding is that the dead in Christ are believers who are alive with Him in heaven and will share with the angels and archangels of heaven in the triumphant return of Christ. Then they will lead the way and "rise first" into heaven, and those who are still physically alive will follow the procession.

The most important teaching of this passage, along with others in the New Testament, is that Christ will return and call believers to Himself. The events that follow this are explained differently by various theological groups. The premillenialist explanation of the last things is that the rapture union with Christ will be followed by seven years of tribulation in which Satan will have sway over the earth in the absence of believers. The Great Tribulation will be marked by immense travail caused by the devices of evil men and the devil. At the end of this period will be the millennium spoken of in Revelation 20. Christ will reign on earth for a thousand years with His saints. This is what is called the premillennialist explanation of the last things.

Not every one holds this point of view. There are the postmillennialists who believe that conditions will progressively improve until we have a utopian era on earth. Christian teaching and preaching is supposed to bring this era of peace and tranquility. The more conservative of the postmillennialists believe that Christ will come after a paradise on earth is established. The difference between the pre- and post- millennialists is that the former believe that Christ will return prior to the millennium and the latter believe that He will return after the humanly induced period of paradise resulting from evolved development of the Kingdom of God on earth.

There is still another group which doesn't believe in the millennium at all. It is made up of those called amillennialists who discount or discredit the Revelation 20 account of the end times. They believe that if there is a thousand-year reign at all, it will be in heaven and not on earth. They hold that the thousand-year time is symbolic and not an actual duration of time. Many, however, believe in a visible, personal return of Christ with judgment.

I would call my own position promillennialist. I'm for it! Since all human prognostication is inadequate, I dare not lean on anything beyond what the Scriptures reveal: Christ will return, the curtain of history as we know it will close. Christ Himself told about the calling out of the world those who belong to Him. Paul describes this pointedly, pictorially, vividly in the passage we are considering. Revelation 20 teaches both the tribulation and the millennium following that. And after that? An eternity with the Lord not measured in years. That's enough for me. All I want to be sure of is that I'll be ready. Any day is possible; no day is impossible. I want to live every day as if it were the last day.

That's the impact of Paul's counsel to the Thessalonians in chapter 5:1-11. He reminds them that no one needs to teach them about "the times and the seasons." Two Greek words for time are used. *Chronos* is an extended period of time and *kairos* is an event-oriented, definite space of time. The apostle seems to be saying, "No one needs to teach you concerning whether the end will be a long time away or whether it will be a spectacular invasion at a specific time." They had been taught that the end of the world will not be the result of evolved human perfection. It will be like a thief in the night. Unexpected, intruding, demanding. A *kairos* event indeed!

Suddenly Paul changes his metaphors. The end will also be like "labor pains on a pregnant woman." The birth of the child cannot be delayed. This metaphor is exciting to contemplate. We must not press it beyond what the apostle intended. But I have often wondered why he utilized a positive image to follow the negative one of the thief in the night. A thief is a fearsome intruder, a child is a welcome gift. Could it be that for those who do not know Christ the end is like a thief and for a believer it is a new birth? For us who are in Christ the end times will not be death throes but birth pains of a new stage of our eternal life. Whether at the demise of our physical life or at the return of Christ, the end will be graduation to heaven. We need not fall into fatalism or despair over the end of the world. It will be like a birth to a new level of existence more sublime than we can imagine.

This is the spirit in which Paul encourages the Christians at Thessalonica to live. They are sons of the day! As such they have armor to protect them. The breastplate of faith and love, the helmet of the hope of salvation—the same triplet we dealt with in chapter 2. All dimensions of time are secured: faith in what Christ did, love from what He does, hope for what He will do. This is the armor we wear in what seems to be the last act of history before the curtain falls. We are the Lord's and are secure whenever it comes. As Paul declares, "For God has not appointed us to wrath, but to obtain salvation by our Lord Jesus Christ." Therefore, "whether we wake or sleep [night or day, if the end comes], we [shall] live together with Him" (5:9, 10).

This section of Thessalonians ends with the admonition to comfort and edify each other on the basis of the assurance we have in Christ for the end times. We are to be sure it is real to us. Then we can comfort and teach one another the hope we have in Christ. The Christian fellowship is to be a laboratory of authentic hope.

The church needs to be very clear about the three advents. There is a vitality in churches which preach and teach all three. The condition of world affairs demands a clear proclamation about the end of the world. Not when, but how. We will be held responsible for the omission of the impelling message of Christ's return. The new church for our decade is a church which preaches and believes in Christ crucified and coming. The startling news will awaken a sleeping generation. The assurance of the hand of the Lord's power on the institutional church is also an awesome challenge. Could it be that the reason He is pouring out His power, reviving the church in America, is because the end is near?

We come back to my breakfast friend's question. How can we have hope in a world like this? We can't! Our hope is not in the world or in our efforts to bring the kingdom on earth, but in the Lord Christ who came, comes and is coming. I'm happy to report that my time that morning in the restaurant began a great, new friendship. Subsequently, the man gave his life to Christ and put on the breastplate of faith and love plus the helmet of hope. He's now alive forever. When his physical death comes, it will not be anything more than passing from one stage of eternal life to the next. If the end of the world comes before or after his physical death, he won't miss either the rapture or the millennium or an endless life in glory after that. Do you have that assurance? Why not live today as if it were the last day? What would you do? What would you settle in your relationship with the Lord?

Seven Steps to Spontaneity

First Thessalonians 5:16-22

Do not quench the Spirit.

What is the one word which would personify the kind of person you long to become?

Recently at a meeting on the Holy Spirit, I asked each of the participants to select a word which would articulate the quality of life he or she wanted to live. Throughout the remainder of the meeting we were to refer to each other by the dynamic description we had selected. I was not surprised that most people chose a word which was quite opposite their natural personalities. We claimed the promise that the Holy Spirit would enable us to be the persons we were meant to be. What do you suppose I chose for myself?

When I became a Christian, a profound personality transformation began. My experience of the Holy Spirit, the indwelling Christ, has continued to liberate me to be a free person—free to love myself and others unconditionally. Daily I must surrender my tendency to caution, reserve, and defensiveness. The Lord's gift to me is to help me be able to give myself away. To fall in love with people and involve myself with spendthrift abandon in their needs. I long to be a completely open, ready-for-anything kind of person. I don't want to resist life in any way. If there has been any progress toward this goal, it is because of the moment-by-moment renewal of the Lord's Spirit in me.

Therefore, the name I have selected for myself is the focus of the kind of person the Spirit has envisioned in my imagination. Spontaneous Lloyd!

I am convinced that an authentic sign that we have become the residence of the Holy Spirit is that we are spontaneous. My working definition of spontaneity is openness, freedom, expectancy, willingness to be surprised, and affirmation of the many splendored thing we call life. The basic meaning of the word means "that which is done freely, arising from inherent qualities." Its root is from "out of free will." True spontaneity is the result of surrendering our wills to the indwelling Spirit so that the inherent qualities by which we respond to life are His. There is an uncalculating, unaffected, unbound excitement in us when the Spirit is given complete freedom to express Himself through us. We become "all-signals-go!" people who respond to life's opportunities and challenges with immediacy and intensity. We were meant to be spontaneous!

God has so much more to reveal to us each day. So often we miss the beauty around us and the serendipities offered us because of our fearful effort to defend, protect and preserve ourselves. As a man said, "I have spent all of my life saving myself for something—I don't know what—and have missed the wonderful delight of living while I'm alive." I have determined to do just the opposite. What about you?

One of the most remarkable men I know is Garland Ingraham, the retail vice-president of Sears Roebuck. When I call him on the phone, I know I can expect his enthusiastic greeting, "Hello, this is Gar Ingraham. What can I do for you?" In the world of marketing in which he would have every temptation to become jaundiced, fearful of manipulation, and on guard of being used or misused, Gar has remained spontaneous. He punctuates a conversation with the oft-repeated question, "Why not?" He's no pushover or easy mark. His goals are clearly set. But in all the pressures of his job he has never lost the contagious quality of being open to fresh ideas, new ways of doing the old and tried. He's a leader of a new breed of Christian businessmen whose faith is expressed in an affirmative receptivity to what God is ready and able to do with a company or a community.

The opposite of spontaneity is stagnation. The other day, I came across an alarming document entitled "The Seven Steps to Stagnation."[7] I found more of myself and the institutional church than I wanted to in each of them. Stagnation is an inevitable result of thinking and saying the following:

1. We've never done it that way.
2. We're not ready for that.
3. We're doing alright without it.
4. We tried that once before.
5. It costs too much.
6. That's not our responsibility.
7. It just won't work.

After reading this sevenfold diagnosis of resistance to the new, the innovative, and the different, I asked God to set me free from saying any of them or expressing them in my attitudes. I began to keep a record of the number of times I heard them from Christians. It was astounding! Often, the very people on whom we depend to model life as a great adventure make these steps the charter of their stagnation. That led me to search the Scriptures for the impetus of authentic, Holy Spirit-originated spontaneity. I wanted something more than the reckless irresponsibility some people claim is spontaneity. How could I become truly spontaneous as God had intended me to be?

I found the answer in Paul's admonitions to the Thessalonians, chapter 5:16-22. In bold contrast to the seven steps to stagnation, here are seven steps to spontaneity. Check the extent of your authentic spontaneity on the basis of this seven-way biblical test.

1. Rejoice always.
2. Pray without ceasing.
3. In everything give thanks;
   for this is the will of God for you.
4. Do not quench the Spirit.
5. Do not despise prophecies.
6. Test all things; hold fast to what is good.
7. Abstain from every form of evil.

As we have noted in each of our expositions in previous chapters, there is a jugular, key verse which is the fulcrum of all the rest. In my opinion, verse 19 unlocks the meaning and might of all the rest of this passage. "Do not quench the Spirit." I want to put this exhortation first and look at the meaning of all the rest in the light of the illuminating splendor of its resources. On the basis of that reordering, which I feel complements the impact the apostle intended, allow me to suggest a contemporary interpretation of these seven strides to spontaneous living. Then I want to share what each can mean in your life and mine for today's incredible opportunities.

1. Accept the gift of enthusiasm.
2. Welcome life expectantly.
3. Dare to be an open person.
4. Thank God for what He will do.
5. Consider the future as a friend.
6. Set courageous goals.
7. Overcome the negative each day by doing a specific, positive good.

Spontaneity is the result of the fire of the Holy Spirit in us. *The first step to spontaneous living is to feed that fire with complete trust. "Don't quench the fire!"* Paul tells us. The implication of the Greek is "Don't develop a habit of quenching the Spirit." The word "quench," when used of fire, means to extinquish, to smother, or stifle. Paul does not mean that we can diminish the Spirit of God, but we can extinguish the fire He builds in our hearts or in others. The only way fire can be extinguished is by something outside itself. The apostle is concerned about anything which hinders the free flow of the Spirit in us or in the Christian fellowship.

When the fires of the Holy Spirit are fueled by our willingness, there is an uncontainable enthusiasm for the gospel, our new life in Christ, people, and the wonder of life. Enthusiasm is the key to great living.

Authentic enthusiasm is a gift. It is not the result of human effort. Many of us have tried on our own strength to become enthusiastic people, only to find that we run out of steam. When our enthusiasm is motivated by people, circumstances, or possibilities we are easily disappointed and become negative. It's not easy to always be sunny, on top, full of excitement.

What then is the secret of a consistent flow of enthusiasm? The fire of the Holy Spirit! Genuine enthusiasm has its unquestionable origin in the indwelling blaze of the Spirit's living in us. Samuel Chadwick, British preacher (1860-1932), said, "Men ablaze are invincible." And I would add, irresistible . . . spontaneous.

The indomitable enthusiasm of the early church was the result of Pentecost. We should not be surprised. John the Baptist predicted it. "I indeed baptize you with water to repentance, but He who is coming after me is mightier than I, whose sandals I am not worthy to carry. He will baptize you with the Holy Spirit and fire" (Matt. 3:11). Then John goes on to clarify an initial and essential result of this Spirit-infused fire. It will mean purification. "His winnowing fan is in His hand, and He will thoroughly purge His threshing floor, and gather His wheat into the barn; but He will burn up the chaff with unquenchable fire" (v. 12). I am convinced that this awesome promise not only has implications for dividing the chaff—those who refused the offer of eternal life in the Saviour—from the wheat—those who heard and responded gladly, but also for the burning up of the chaff in each of us who has become His disciple. The fire of the Holy Spirit burns out of us the chaff of pride, self-will, and fear. The winnowing fan drives off the chaff from the wheat in us and burns it with an unquenchable fire.

The Greek word for enthusiasm is *enthusiasmos,* meaning "in God," or "inspired by God." When we become Spirit-filled people, the fire of the Spirit burns out anything which would keep us cold, cautious or constricted. That's why I say enthusiasm is a gift. It is God's own life-affirming, creative, positive Spirit, who cleanses and then charges us with uncontainable excitement for living.

The identifiable, outward manifestation of the fire of Pentecost burning in us is willingness and warmth. James S. Stewart of Edinburgh was right: "The supreme need of the church is the same in the twentieth century as in the first; it is men on fire for Christ." Enthusiasm for Christ will make us wide open to people and the immense possibilities offered in each relationship. Resistance to life will be replaced by receptivity.

Then we will be ready for *the second step to spontaneous living. Rejoice always.* That, for me, means to welcome life with expectancy. We can tackle all that life offers if we can praise God for what happens to and around us. The delight and the difficult; the routine and the serendipitous. The key to unlocking both the challenge and the concern of life is to rejoice with enthusiasm. This is not simplistic sentimentalism. It is rooted in a profound trust that God can use everything. We will discover new truth and advance through life's pleasant and painful experiences. When disappointment or setbacks hit us they all contain a hidden joy. We can wade into impossibilities with enthusiasm because we have learned that our most pressing problems in the past have forced us to learn two essential lessons from life: (1) God is in charge, and (2) we have grown most when we've trusted Him in spite of difficulties.

Rejoicing enables us to embrace the ups and downs of life without reservation. When we expect to discover truth and growth from each person or circumstance, we are not disappointed.

While I was studying this passage, I had an experience which brought home the truth of "rejoice always." I had spent an entire day dictating responses to letters on my dictating machine. Each letter was composed with utmost care. Our church's television ministry has multiplied my correspondence and I try to be faithful in personally acknowledging prayer requests sent to me and gifts for the ministry. The tape was full of such communications.

After I finished, I put the tape in a folder to take to my office to give to my administrative assistant for typing and sending. Somewhere between the place where I had hidden away to get caught up on my mail and my office, the tape was lost! I was frantic to find it because of all the work. Hours of searching were unrewarded. Then it hit me: could I rejoice? Not easily. But following the advice I'd been writing in this chapter, I dared to rejoice that some good could come out of this goof.

A day later I realized that a couple of the letters I had dictated were far from maximum responses to the needs addressed to me. I was able to do them over. But the significant thing was that rejoicing gave me release from the tension of the foolish loss of the tape.

We all face trivial and momentous difficulties which will either destroy our effectiveness or enable us to let go of the frustration and pick up the broken pieces and start again. That can happen only if we rejoice that God can use everything for our growth and His glory.

I know a man who keeps a journal of each day's discoveries. At the end of each day, he writes down what God has taught him. He believes it's not the number of breaths we breathe but the number of breath-taking experiences each day offers. After a long period of resisting life, he has been liberated to expect the miracles of God in his daily life. He doesn't want to forget any of them. That's the reason he writes them down daily: he wants to be fortified to begin the next day with spontaneity.

The only way to take this crucial step to spontaneous living is to try it. Make this week a seven-day experiment. Resolve to rejoice! Not regardless of what comes your way, but because of it. There's a blessing waiting, wrapped up in each questionable eventuality. Expect it. Look for it. Thank God for it in advance. You will note the change that happens in your attitudes.

This second step is inseparably related to the third. We can rejoice because we are ready to learn what God is saying to us in all of life. *Paul's secret of power in all circumstances is to "pray without ceasing."* Prayer is cumulative friendship with the Lord. It gives us perspective on what life brings. Spontaneous prayer is moment by moment checking in with the Lord for His direction. When we are completely open to life we can ask, "Okay Lord, what are you going to do with this problem or potential? I believe you work all things together for good. What's next on your agenda for me in this?"

The great thing about praying constantly is that it keeps us open channels for what the Lord wants to accomplish in every situation. Instead of being thrown by changes, we can throw ourselves into making changes according to His guidance. Authentic spontaneity comes from this consistent companionship of prayer.

We can pray quietly inside in every situation: when we are alone or with people; when we are reflective or deeply involved in pressure. We are never alone! Thoreau said, "Most men lead lives of quiet desperation." Not so for the constantly praying Christian.

I have a friend who has a favorite saying. She says, "I'm in complete control. It's the situation that's out of hand." I don't agree. We were never meant to be in complete control—the Lord is; and then the situation can be surrendered to Him with complete confidence that He will use all that happens. He gives us tread in the midst of trouble. The valley of troubles becomes a door of hope (see Hos. 2:15, *TLB*).

Two memory verses from the Psalms have helped me live spontaneously in trouble. One is Psalm 27:1 (*TLB*), "The Lord is my light and my salvation; whom shall I fear?" Another is Psalm 56:3,4 (*TLB*), "But when I am afraid, I will put my confidence in you. Yes, I will trust the promises of God. And since I am trusting him, what can mere man do to me?"

Another great advantage of praying constantly is that we can dare to live in the now. Life moves swiftly. It's easy to collect debilitating memories, hurts, and resentments. Our spontaneity is blocked by the collection of garbage in our souls. When we are in persistent conversation with God we can deal with the feelings immediately. The next hour does not need to be polluted by the unresolved attitudes of the past hour. We can get rid of the past before it becomes part of the present. I remember when I was a radio announcer a mistake or mispronounced word, what we called a "fluff," had to be forgotten immediately or it would ruin a whole half-hour program with repeated mistakes.

The very positive side of praying constantly is the birth of creative anticipation. Before and during an encounter or opportunity, we can pray for the Lord's instant guidance. He has promised to replace our sagacity with wisdom, our analysis with discernment, our insight with inspiration. Life in the Spirit is like stepping into the fast moving currents of a river. We are carried along by supernatural power. "There is a river whose streams make glad the city of God" (Ps. 46:4).

When my son Andrew and I traveled throughout the

Orient visiting missionaries, we faced the pressure of plane schedules and a constant flow of speaking engagements. We claimed the assurance of the river of the Spirit. Often Andy would slip up beside me and whisper in my ear, "Float, Dad, float!" The reminder kept me spontaneous to each propitious opportunity.

I've always had the conviction in administration that if two people are doing the same job in an organization, one of them is unnecessary. The same would be true of our relationship to God. If He and I are trying to do the task of running the universe, I am duplicating His responsibility. My job description as a Christian is to pray constantly, discover God's will, and be an implementor by obediently following orders. When I get out of line and assume God's self-delineated job description, I take onto myself authority which is not mine. Added to that, I don't have the wisdom and omniscience to tackle that job! I was never meant to. I play God when I do.

Prayer without ceasing is becoming a recipient of power for life. We are all over our heads with problems we can't solve and people's needs we can't meet. The Lord has promised to give us what we need. I find that by imagining my mind, emotions and will as a channel through which the Holy Spirit can move freely, He will infuse thoughts beyond my understanding and love beyond my capability. True freedom comes when we know that He will be punctual with exactly what's needed in each situation. But He will not flow through us unless we open the floodgates. Tennyson described the meaning of praying constantly when he said, "Prayer is like opening a sluice between a great ocean and our little channels, when the sea gathers itself together and flows at full tide."[8]

The next step, to thank God, is given special emphasis by Paul. "In everything give thanks; for this is the will of God in Christ Jesus for you." Thankful prayer is not an option, it is God's will. He knows that no difficult situation or problem person is released to Him until we give Him thanks. Ambrose of Milan said, "No duty is more urgent than that of returning thanks." We become spontaneous to the extent that we have become thankful for what has and is happening to us. We become open to further blessings when we thank God. Andrew Murray, South African missionary and educator (1828-1917), knew this. "To be thankful for what we have received, and for what my Lord has prepared, is the surest way to receive more." Sin is really ingratitude.

The other day I called a friend with a disappointing report on a project. "I'm afraid I have some bad news for you," I said.

"Thank God!" he responded immediately.

"What?" I said astoundedly.

"Well," he said thoughtfully, "I want what God wants. If the report is less than what I hoped then I am thankful because to have something He has not willed would not be best for me. To have what He wills is joy; to have something He has not willed is spiritual suicide. Give me the report and let's move on from here. "We've got to be ready to play the ball where it is on the field," he added with vibrant spontaneity.

Thanksgiving also engenders spontaneity in positive blessings. We all need to know that what we have and are is a gift. Success can cripple spontaneity more quickly than failure or problems. We begin to think that we accomplished it ourselves. Soon we clutch life tightly to assure a continuous flow of victories. We are in danger of losing our freedom after a series of successes. When we take the credit because of cleverness or hard work we get tense trying to stay on top. Only gratitude can break the bind. John Henry Jowett said, "Every virtue divorced from thankfulness is maimed and limps along the spiritual road."

When our life is one constant "Thank you, Lord," we are liberated from imperious self-control. A thankful heart is the parent of authentic spontaneity. I want to enjoy my gifts as much as I do the beauty of the natural world, knowing that I did nothing to earn or deserve either.

The truly spontaneous people I know are thankful people. Like the one out of ten healed lepers who returned to the Master to express gratitude, they are ready for the fresh blessing or challenge of the Lord because they have thanked Him for His provision in both the valleys and mountaintops of life. My old professor, the late John Baillie, used to put it to us students this way: "Gratitude is not only the dominant note in Christian piety, but equally the dominant motive of Christian action. Such gratitude is for the grace that has been shown us by God. A true Christian is a person who never for a moment forgets what God has done for him in Christ, and whose whole comportment and whole activity have their root in the sentiment of gratitude."

This moves us on to the next step to spontaneous living. When we are filled with gratitude for the past and all that God has taught us in success or failure, *we can accept the future as a friend.* A spontaneous person knows that God gives the day and shows the way. As we said earlier in our study of growth, there is still undiscovered truth for us to learn and experience. Each new phase of life will show us more of the Lord and more of ourselves.

Paul admonished, "Do not despise prophecies" (1 Thess. 5:20). In 1 Corinthians 14, he singled out prophecy as one of the chief spiritual gifts. Prophetic utterance had great authority in the early church. Prophets were equivalent to preachers. The word in Greek for "prophecies" is *prophēterias* meaning forth-telling more than fore-telling. Often they blend together. A forth-telling of truth is a fore-telling of how we must act in the future to live out a truth. We know only as much as we have enacted in our daily lives. Truth is known when it's done and done when it's known.

The thing the Lord seems to be asking me in response to Paul's admonition is, "Lloyd, are you open and ready for new truth? Are you willing to keep on learning? There is so much you have not discovered. Keep open to the future. It is filled with revelations from Me that will astound you with how little you know!"

What can I say to that except, "I'm ready, Lord, pour it on!"

The reliable test that we are not quenching the Holy Spirit is that we are more excited about the future than we are about the past. Great churches are made up of people who long to press on into the deeper dimensions of the Word of God. I am always encouraged by the "Press on!" look on the faces of my Hollywood congregation. Preaching to them is more than a forensic exchange of ideas. They come to worship as men and women thirsty for the Water of Life. The battle of faith, hope and love in the world has made them famished for the Bread of Life. The future is not an enemy; it's a friend which greets them with the promise of new impossibilities which the Lord will use to teach them more of His power to change impossibilities into possibilities.

The next step in Paul's delineation seems strangely negative. Not so! *We are to test all things and hold fast to what is good* (see 1 Thess. 5:21). Spontaneous living is not being open to do whatever the whim of the moment dictates. Spontaneity is freedom to respond to what God has guided. For me, Paul's exhortation means to know what is good according to God's plan for you and move forward to prayerfully-established goals to accomplish it. Clearly defined goals are to the spontaneous person what sails are to a boat. They catch and concentrate the wind of the Spirit. They also help us to know what is maximum for us. We can quickly decide between alternatives and be positive in moving forward.

I believe in ten-year, five-year, three-year, one-year, and one-month goals. I can respond to or reject opportunities on the basis of my one-month goals in the light of my short- and long-range goals. The reason many of us get frustrated and lose our spontaneity is because we don't know where we are going. True freedom is always expressed within carefully defined limits. No great literature or art was ever produced by a person who worked when he felt like it. No profound romantic love has been expressed to several among many. Choices must be made. Creativity is concentrated power from the Holy Spirit.

I know a man who takes a 72-hour period every year to be absolutely alone with God. The first 24 hours are spent getting thoroughly quiet. He cleanses his soul with forgiveness and grace. His mind is centered on God and all that He has been and done. The next 24 hours are spent envisioning where God wants him to be in 10 years. What are the Lord's goals and priorities? He writes them down carefully as prayer releases the flow. The gift of imagination focuses the image. He actually lives out in his mind the vision of 10 years hence. The last 24 hours are spent writing an "action description" of the steps to be taken in each of the 12 months of the year ahead. My friend leaves his retreat refreshed and determined. He knows what to say yes to and when to say no! He is spontaneous.

At the beginning of each month, he writes out what he must do in those 30 days to move forward to his one-year goals in the context of his ten-year plan. I had often wondered why he was so free of pressure. When he told me how he learned to envision the Lord's will for his life, I found the secret of his effectiveness.

We all need a basis of testing all things and holding fast to what is good. The word for "good" in Paul's admonition is *kalon* from *kalos,* meaning noble, beautiful, winsome, and attractive. There are two words for "good" in Greek. The other is *agathos* which simply defines a thing as good in quality. *Kalos* is so much more. Goodness is an attribute of God. It defines His consistency and faithfulness to His nature of pure love. He can be depended on to be true to His revealed nature of unfailing grace revealed in Jesus Christ.

In that light, the good is that which is consistent with God's plan and purpose for us in Christ. We have an irreducible maximum for our primary goals. What will help us grow to the measure of the stature of the fullness of Christ? What will make us more like Him in word, action, attitude, and spirit? What will further the Kingdom in our lives—that is, His reign and rule? Once we answer these questions we can move on to secondary goals. What particular task has He called us to do? Where will we be in 10 years in accomplishing the specific thing each of us, and no other, was born to do? Both the primary and secondary goals are part of the "good" for us. We are called to be unique miracles of our Lord.

There are few things which give life more verve than knowing "what is that good and acceptable and perfect will of God" (Rom. 12:2) in the short- and long-range goals of our lives. We know where we are headed and can react with spontaneity to everything which brings us closer to our destiny and destination as persons. And the Holy Spirit will guide us each step of the way!

Some time ago Lawrence A. Appley, chairman of the board of the American Management Association gave an outstanding speech in Akron, Ohio. Afterward, he opened the meeting for questions. A bright young student asked, "Mr. Appley, what are your 10-year goals?"

To this he replied, "Do you know how old I am? I am 75." The young man acknowledged that he knew that and asked his question again. The experience thundered home to the great leader the fresh realization that we are never too old to have a daring dream.

Now we are ready to consider the positive action of step seven. *We are free to spontaneously overcome the negative by doing a specific good.* How else can we consistently "abstain from every form of evil"? Paul articulates the secret in Romans 12:21: "Do not be overcome by evil, but overcome evil with good."

Evil for most of us is simply a distortion of the good. It is anything which, when done, separates us from God, other people, and our true selves. Satan is constantly trying to lead us astray or beguile us with the treason of the right thing for the wrong reason or the wrong thing for a right reason. Evil is fundamentally rebellion. It is using the gifts of God to run our own or others' lives. The Ten Commandments have not gone out of style. Jesus' Great Commandment to love is as irrevocable today as it was 2,000 years ago. We don't break those commandments; we break ourselves on them.

Surely Paul was referring to the pagan way of life in Thessalonica when he called the new Christians to abstain from every form of evil. He called for purity. The same distortions of sex, marriage, the family and the dignity of personhood are around today. But then, as now, every evil, rebellious contradiction of what God intended life to be must be replaced by a creative affirmation of His will for us. We fall into the trap of evil by the vacuum left in our souls. A life focused on Christ, a will determined to discern and do His will, and action which incarnates His guidance fills that vacuum.

Think of it in terms of the desire for retribution. When we are hurt we want to hurt back. The temptation to return evil for evil is always present. The spontaneous person does not quench the Holy Spirit's nudging to take the first step to bring reconciliation. He or she is guided by Jesus' admonition, "I say to you, love your enemies, bless those who curse you, do good to those who hate you, and pray for those who spitefully use you and persecute you, that you may be sons of your Father who is in heaven" (Matt. 5:44,45). What better description could there be for overcoming evil?

Our temptation to evil always has a flip side. What is the opposite of the evil, rebellious, hurting thing? Do that and the bind is broken.

The opposite of evil is love—for God, ourselves, and others. It is lack of healthy self-love and esteem that prompts us to do anything which will fracture those relationships. When we allow God to love us more profoundly, our own self-esteem grows. It is then that we can think through what will bring the ultimate good and do it spontaneously. Abstinence from evil is possible only by absolute obedience. What is the opposite of the evil thing you are tempted to do or say today? Do that before the day is done and you will have won!

Well, there you have the seven steps to spontaneous living under the guidance of the Holy Spirit. They are all inter- twined. One leads on to the next. Dare to take an incisive inventory of how spontaneous a person you have allowed the Holy Spirit to make you. Turn back to our seven steps listed on page 92. Place a number from 0 to 5 beside each. Put a 0 if you have not experienced any one of the steps or 1 to 5 for your evaluation of the extent you have. Now total your score: 35? Anything less defines our marching orders for today. The Holy Spirit is ready to make us authentically spon- taneous! And why not?

8

Wholeness for the Fragmatic

First Thessalonians 5:23, 24

*Now may the God of peace Himself sanctify you
completely; and may your whole spirit, soul, and
body be preserved blameless at the coming of our
Lord Jesus Christ. He who calls you is faithful,
who also will do it.*

There's a boy in my congregation who shares my love for
words. He tries to stump me with the challenge to spell and
define new words he's discovered. To my dismay—and a few
times embarrassment—he's come up with some words that I
didn't know were in the dictionary, and a few others, I later
found out, were not. Like some adults, he gets the wrong
word in the right place or a right word in the wrong place.

Recently he led me down a primrose path of conversation
to set me up for the use of a word he'd learned (or so he
thought!). He asked me if I knew a word based on a Latin
word to describe a person who is active or skilled in practical
affairs. While I thought, he added that it also was used for the
scientific evolution of causes and effects. Before I could say
the word, he said, "I'm a very fragmatic person you know!" He
meant pragmatic. We both laughed when I explained the

difference; but I thanked him for coining a new word.

A "fragmatic" person! The phrase describes many of us and what's happening to us. We are scattered people, flying off in all directions. But the problem is more profound than the pressure of too much to do or a multiplicity of competing loyalties. We are "fragmatic" in our nature. The unity of mind, soul, emotion, will and body has been wrenched apart. We long to be made whole as we were meant to be. The explosion of man's nature, begun in Adam's rebellion against God, is still detonating, sending the shrapnel of our persons in every direction.

Perhaps this is the reason there is so much talk about wholeness today. Physicians are discovering that they must treat the whole person and have developed what's called holistic medicine. Eminent internists at long last are investigating the deeper causes of some sickness in the mental and spiritual dis-ease of patients. Oncologists are busy these days plumbing the depths of the interrelationship of stress and some forms of cancer. Psychiatrists are becoming aware that you can't heal emotional disorders without remedial care for a person's body, spirit, relationships and environment. Theologians are finally showing a reverence for more than conceptualized belief and are devoting time to the implications of right thinking for emotional health and relational integration.

Spiritual leaders have had to face the fact that many people who are "saved" are still emotional cripples who need the healing of memories or the liberation of their wills to act on what they believe. It is an exciting time of discovering a very basic truth: a human being is a unity. All the person-healing disciplines are realizing that they cannot deal with one aspect of the complex nature of a person without care for the whole person.

The church in this decade is called to be the fellowship of frontiersmen in the breaking of ground in the battle against "fragmation," to build on the young intellectual lad's malapropism. We are called to be a healing community in which people can become whole.

Our word "whole" comes from the Anglo-Saxon word *hal*, meaning whole, completeness, or integration. As we noted in our earlier chapter on sanctification, holiness and wholeness come from the same root. The focus of this chapter is to consider the source of wholeness, the substantive elements of wholeness, and the surety of wholeness. Paul's closing blessing to the Thessalonians in 5:23, 24 provides us a biblical basis of our outline of thought. "Now may the God of peace Himself sanctify you completely; and may your whole spirit, soul, and body be preserved blameless at the coming of our Lord Jesus Christ. He who calls you is faithful, who also will do it."

①The source of wholeness is peace. The Greek word for "peace", *eirēnē*, means more than tranquility or absence of outer conflict. The word implies a knitting together of what has been fragmented. Peace is the Lord's healing of the "fragmatist." It results in the perfect unity of all the factors of our humanity.

Peace is the gift of Calvary. The strife and enmity between God and man caused by sin, has been dealt with in a-once-and-for-all, complete atonement. Peace is made between God and those who will accept the free gift of forgiveness, reconciliation and love through the blood of the cross. There is no hope of wholeness until we are reunited with our Lord through the imputed righteousness we have through the Lamb of God, Christ our Sacrifice. When we are pulled apart by rebellion and the arrogant desire to run our own lives, we are fractured from the centering power which can pull us together.

Alienation from God alienates us from ourselves and other people. Self-hate expressed in self-justification and pride eventually leaves us with no anchor for the storms of life. We do not know who we are, where we are going or what is the purpose of our existence. Experiencing the peace of

God through the cross is the beginning of the miracle of becoming a whole person. Until that healing process takes place, we are a walking civil war. Our minds are confused by distorted thought, our emotions become an expression of that lack of direction, our wills are immobilized and our bodies absorb the tension of the broken relationship with the One for whom we were created.

In Romans 7 Paul describes the quest for peace and wholeness with first-person intensity. He understands our plight, he has been there. After the radical turn-around of his conversion, the apostle went through a growing process of becoming a whole person in Christ. The 10 years of solitude in preparation for his ministry was a time of reorientation and healing. He invites us into his turbulent struggle for wholeness both before and after accepting Christ. What he shares is an apt description of our fragmented natures and the hope we can share. *The Living Bible* paraphrase is a vivid, contemporary rendering of the Greek of this passage:

"When I want to do good, I don't; and when I try not to do wrong, I do it anyway. Now if I am doing what I don't want to, it is plain where the trouble is: sin still has me in its evil grasp. It seems to be a fact of life that when I want to do what is right, I inevitably do what is wrong. I love to do God's will so far as my new nature is concerned; but there is something else deep within me, in my lower nature, that is at war with my mind and wins the fight and makes me a slave to the sin that is still within me. In my mind I want to be God's willing servant but instead I find myself still enslaved to sin. So you see how it is: my new life tells me to do right, but the old nature that is still inside me loves to sin. Oh, what a terrible predicament I'm in! Who will free me from my slavery to this deadly lower nature?" (Rom. 7:19-25).

Paul answers his own question (v. 25): "Thank God! It has been done by Jesus Christ our Lord. He has set me free." A footnote rendering in *The Living Bible* says, "It will be done." Both are true in reality. Christ has accomplished it by the cross and it will be done progressively as our total nature grows in the wholeness offered to us in our regeneration. The assurance of that is in the first two verses of chapter 8 of Romans and should be read as a continuation of the thought of chapter seven: "So there is now no condemnation awaiting those who belong to Christ Jesus. For the power of the life-giving Spirit—and this power is mine through Christ Jesus—has freed me from the vicious circle of sin and death" (Rom. 8:1,2, *TLB*).

That circle is broken by Christ as He penetrates and then unifies all facets of our nature. He is at work in us. The growing unity of Paul's nature was the result of dying daily to his own control of his spirit, soul and body so that Christ could transform and integrate him. Christ in him had an ever-increasing victory over the old nature and the resurrection of the new Paul.

A question begs consideration: Why are there so few Christians who are whole? The reason is that many of us have resisted His invasion into all the aspects of our nature. It is possible to believe that Jesus is the Christ and still be a fragmented person. There are conceptual Christians whose faith has not penetrated emotion, will or body. Also there are emotional Christians who need to get their thinking straight as well as volitional Christians who are willing to do what's right without the power to do it. And there are others who need to discover how to express their faith in their physical lives. The body's habits, disabilities or passions must be brought under the control of the Spirit. Instead of being fragmented into pieces, we can know the peace of the harmonious functioning of our total nature under His Lordship. The peace of Christ enables wholeness.

Now move on to the substantive elements of our many-faceted nature. We know we are intellectual, emotional, volitional and physical. We have been endowed with the capacity to think, feel, decide and live physically. We are a quadrilateral creation. All of the delineations of our nature in Scripture encompass all of these, though there are a variety of Hebrew and Greek words used to designate the parts.

Moses called Israel to love the Lord with all their heart, soul and might (see Deut. 6:5). Jesus quoted this description of the capacities of our nature and added "with all your mind" (Matt. 22:37; Mark 12:30). Including "mind" was not to add something that was lacking in the Deuteronomic description, but to stress the commitment of thought as an essential part of loving God. Both Moses and Jesus plainly mean that we are to love and serve God with all our entrusted powers. In the Hebrew understanding of personality the word "heart" encompassed intellect, emotions and will. The "soul" was considered the life verve, the vitality of a person. "Might" denotes the body and the physical strength with which we serve the Lord God. It is important to remember that the Hebrews considered a human being as a unified creation.

Paul stands in this great tradition, but also shows the influence of the Greek understanding of human nature. His prayer for the Thessalonians, for example, is that they will be whole in spirit, soul and body. Investigation of these designations reveals that he really meant all aspects of our nature.

Our spirit, *pneuma*, is the most sublime and distinctive part of our created nature. Unlike all other creatures, we have been given the capacity to know, communicate with and receive the Spirit of God. This is basic in Paul's thought throughout his writings. The blemished spirit of man, distorted by the fall, can be healed and recreated as a result of reconciliation through faith in Christ. Our spirit can be the post-resurrection home of the living Christ, the Holy Spirit.

The "soul," according to Paul, is the self-conscious seat of personality including intellect, emotion and will. He uses the Greek word *psuchē* for our thinking, feeling, deciding capacities. The word is used extensively throughout the New Testament: 48 times as soul, 40 times as life, three times as

mind and once as heart. I am convinced that Paul uses it in
this Thessalonian passage very much as the Deuteronomy
passage uses heart for thought, emotion and will. The inclusion of both spirit and soul was not a careless, redundant
coupling of synonyms. Paul wanted the Thessalonians to
claim the capacity to know and receive God's Spirit, as well as
become responsible in exercising their full intellectual, emotional and volitional potential as an expression of their faith.

3) The third part of the trichotomy of the substantive elements of our nature is the body, *sōma*. Paul was concerned
about the physical health and purity of the body. Our spirits
and souls dwell in our bodies; and the Holy Spirit dwells in
our spirits and utilizes our souls to inspire our thoughts,
engender our emotions and guide our wills. For Paul, the
body is the temple of the Holy Spirit. He called for reverence
and care of the body as holy, sacred, set apart to glorify God.
"Do you not know that your body is the temple of the Holy
Spirit who is in you, whom you have from God, and you are
not your own? For you were bought at a price [Calvary];
therefore glorify God in your body and in your spirit, which
are God's" (1 Cor. 6:19, 20).

The total impact of Paul's prayer for the *eirēnē* unification of the Thessalonians' spirit, soul and body is essentially
the same as Moses and Jesus. He longed for completeness in
all facets of our nature; for our spirit, soul and body to march
to the same drummer in a harmonious glorification of God in
all of life.

"Now may the God of peace Himself sanctify you completely; and may your whole spirit, soul, and body be preserved blameless" (1 Thess. 5:23) is his salient supplication.
We move closer to an understanding of wholeness when we
plumb the depths of the words "complete" and "whole."
These two compound Greek words, set in juxtaposition in
Paul's prayer for the Thessalonians, give us two vital aspects
of wholeness. The word for "completely," *holoteleis*, is a combination of *holos*, meaning "whole, entire" and *telos*, mean-

ing "end, goal, purpose." The word for "whole" in the next part of the sentence ("whole spirit, soul, and body") is *holok-lēron*—a combination of *holos,* "whole" and *kleros,* meaning "lot; a portion delegated by lot; calling." Putting the meaning of "completely" and "whole" together, what Paul seems to be praying is that the Thessalonians' entire spirits, souls and bodies be freely open, committed, receptive and utilized for the purpose of each part's calling, and that they all work in unity to accomplish the purpose of the total life of the Christian.

We long for the same wholeness Paul wanted for the Thessalonians. His prayer articulates an antidote to the fragmentation we feel. We need a spirit filled with Christ's Spirit, a soul infused with wisdom and discernment, emotional health and freedom of will; and a body radiant with physical strength and soundness. But we yearn for something more—that under the control of the indwelling Christ, the sublime unifier, we would experience greater oneness in these dimensions of our nature.

③ Now note the surety of this wholeness. "He who calls you is faithful, who also will do it" (v. 24). The Lord will finish what He has begun. Faithfulness is a part of the essential nature of the Lord. We join the psalmist in gratitude for the rock of His faithfulness on which we stand. "Praise the Lord, all nations; laud Him, all peoples! For His lovingkindness is great toward us, and the truth [faithfulness] of the Lord is everlasting. Praise the Lord!" (Ps. 117:1, 2). Faithfulness describes the Lord's consistency, integrity and punctuality in intervening in our lives to bring growth in our total nature through all of life's ups and downs. My favorite verses about the faithfulness of God are Lamentations 3:21-26. Jeremiah recalls the Lord's unwavering help in excruciating circumstances which freed the prophet to grow as a man of faith. Remembering all he had been through and what God had done for him Jeremiah says,

This I recall to my mind,
Therefore I have hope.
The Lord's lovingkindnesses indeed never cease,
For His compassions never fail.
They are new every morning;
Great is Thy faithfulness.
"The Lord is my portion," says my soul,
"Therefore I have hope in Him."
The Lord is good to those who wait for Him,
To the person who seeks Him.
It is good that he waits silently
For the salvation of the Lord.

Paul believed and lived in that assurance of the Lord's faithfulness. The same faithfulness revealed in the Incarnation, the cross, Pentecost and Christ's presence would be expressed consistently in the growth of wholeness in the Thessalonians. They could count on it, says Paul. And so can we. The assurance he gave the Ephesians in a later letter, he seems to communicate to the struggling Christians of Thessalonica. He wanted them to "come to the unity of the faith and the knowledge of the Son of God, to a perfect man, to the measure of the stature of the fullness of Christ; that we should no longer be children, tossed to and fro and carried about with every wind of doctrine, by the trickery of men, in the cunning craftiness by which they lie in wait to deceive, but, speaking the truth in love, may grow up in *all things* into Him who is the head—Christ—from whom the whole body, joined and knit together by what every joint supplies, according to the effective working by which every part does its share, causes growth of the body for the edifying of itself in love" (Eph. 4:13-16).

The image of the body with its many parts often is used by Paul to describe how the various aspects of our nature are to work together in wholeness. And the Lord is faithful to perform it. He will not leave us "fragmatic" people. His holistic work in us is to maximize us in spirit, soul and body.

Here is how He does it. He works continuously in each of the three parts of our nature which Paul delineates and then brings them into an ever-increasing unity. *Wholeness starts with our spirits.* The magna carta for our spiritual growth is in Jesus' words, "God is Spirit, and those who worship Him must worship Him in spirit and truth" (John 4:24). There are two uses of the Greek word for spirit in this passage. The one referring to God is *pneuma,* and the word for the spirit of a person is *pneumati.* Our spirit is the God-intended contact point with Him. He created us for fellowship with Him. Since He is Spirit, He has made us capable of knowing Him, experiencing His love and enjoying a faithful friendship with Him. Our spirits were meant to be His home. The impact of Christ's life, death, resurrection and return in the Holy Spirit was to launch a new creation, a new breed of humanity to fulfill God's original intention of creating a people to be His people.

Our spirits are the control center of the new life in Christ. Wholeness is begun when we yield our spirits to be filled with His Spirit. He begins His renovation process in our spirits and is never finished until He has refashioned us completely in His likeness. Our first step to wholeness is to yield our spirits to His indwelling power and control.

The next step is with our souls. Remember we defined the soul, *psuchē,* as the composite of intellect, emotion and will. Christ makes a beachhead in our spirits and then penetrates into souls, capturing our understanding, healing and liberating our emotions and reorienting our wills to do His will. To be whole in our soul is to surrender our minds to be the thinking agent of Christ. We are to be intellectual Christians who express the mind of Christ in our thinking, understanding and the concepts which guide our living and relationships. William Durant was too close to being right for comfort when he said that too many Christians check their intellects with their coats when they come to church. And I would add, also when we live our daily lives. Most of us are using one-tenth of the intellectual power given to us. We tolerate sloppy thinking in our affairs. We avoid thinking through the deeper truth of the gospel in the sticky issues of life.

Thoughtful meditation is a part of prayer. The Spirit will guide us in comprehending His plan and purpose in history. He will invade our misunderstanding with insight and clarity we could not achieve ourselves. It does not take a genius to be a Christian, but it takes all the intellect we have. Some of us need to be converted intellectually as well as spiritually. Many Christians stopped thinking, rather than began when they were converted. The plea for the simple gospel is an evasion. The basic truth of God's love and forgiveness is simple indeed, but the vastness of His providence and plan is profound and demands our intellectual best. The study of the Scriptures requires a committed, receptive mind. Sorting out God's strategy with clearly defined goals requires all our intelligence, infused with wisdom from the Lord. Communicating our faith stretches us to have initiative and be innovative in figuring out how to answer the tough intellectual questions which keep people from accepting the faith.

I know a man who has given up the Christian life because his conversion did not capture his mind. Years after his heartwarming experience of salvation, he was forced to confront intellectual issues which plummeted him into doubt. His church had failed him in not forcing him to become an intellectual disciple. Intellectual infantilism is a major cause of an inept church. We all need Paul's bracing word to the Corinthians, many of whom were languishing on a plateau of intellectual self-satisfaction. "Brethren, do not be children in understanding . . . but in understanding be mature" (1 Cor. 14:20). Wholeness is loving God with our minds!

The same is true for our emotions. The process of growth in Christ penetrates into our emotional nature. Our feelings about the past hurts of life need the healing of our memories.

How we react emotionally in the present must be surrendered to the momentary guidance of the Spirit in our souls. There's no such thing as an unexpressed emotion. If our feelings are suppressed, they come out in some other way. Emotional maturity requires an honest examination of our feelings and reactions. Either our minds control our emotions or our emotions dominate our thinking.

God has created us with the awesome capacity to feel. We can feel love or hate, joy or discouragement, warmth or hostility, delight or depression, acceptance or anger, trust or fear, pity or praise. Emotional wholeness is bringing our feelings under the guidance of the mind of Christ. His mind in us sends the right signals into our emotions and helps us to respond as He would in any situation. We grow in emotional wholeness when we bring every feeling to Him for His refortification or healing.

A mature, whole Christian can honestly open himself to Christ's scrutiny and liberating love. We do not need to be immature, flying off the handle, doing what the feeling of the moment demands. We don't have to spend the rest of our lives as emotional spastics. Old hurts do not need to be misdirected at people today. Resentments toward people can be transformed. The same emotional channel used for fear can be inundated with a flow of love from Christ in us. Christ wants to make us whole emotionally.

Closely related to our emotions is the will. This is our capacity to decide. Volitionally whole Christians persistently surrender their wills to know and do the Lord's will. We constantly face decisions for which we need His guidance. Our character can be the result of a completely Christ-fashioned will. Jesus' insistence that we worship with spirit and truth is the key. When He takes up residence in our spirits, His truth invades our minds and becomes the basis of our deciding. Truth must be obeyed if we are to be whole persons. Any truth which is not acted on, actually becomes a detriment to further growth in wholeness. When an insight is not lived, it is worse than a chance lost; it works negatively to hinder future resolutions and implementation of thought.

Jesus exemplified a surrendered will and called candidates for the new creation who would eventually demonstrate in history what volitional obedience was meant to be in God's original purpose for His people. The Lord's persistent prayer was "not My will, but Thine be done" and affirmed those whose will was to do His Father's will. Luther was right: "Those who believe, obey and those who obey, believe." Belief and action are one in a whole person. Behavior is never fragmented from conviction.

The next aspect of Paul's trichotomy is the body. Our physical nature is to be a glory to God. Paul shared with the Philippians his prayer that he might always magnify Christ in his body. The effective functioning of the body has a telling impact on our spirits and minds. A commitment to Christ includes care for our bodies. The body can either impede or assist our life in Christ. We are responsible as stewards of our physical health. Nutrition, exercise, rest and recreation are Christian disciplines as well as prayer, study and witnessing. The neglect of the body is a contradiction to our faith. Though the body is left behind when we move on to the heavenly stage of our eternal life, what we do with our bodies in the years of life on earth should be an expression of our indwelling Lord in our spirits.

Lack of rest and exercise can debilitate our discipleship. A physically exhausted Christian is an irritable, testy tool for the Lord to use. Obesity is a megaphone shout to the world that we are out of control. Compulsive habits deny our commitment.

The body is not bad. When God created us, He said it was good. The body can be a God-given source of pleasure, delight, satisfaction, and self-esteem. Our physical nature is the sacred dwelling place of our spirit and soul.

Jesus spent a great deal of His ministry caring for the bodies of people. He healed and commissioned the church with the power to heal. He knew that the wholeness which God intended included the body. And yet we live in a world of germs and disease. But there is a name for healing greater than the evil of sickness: Jesus Christ. In His name, His healing is released in our bodies, not just for our comfort, but for active discipleship. Christ is the healing power of the world. Medical science can remove obstructions and utilize the discoveries of pharmacology, but the Lord does the healing.

The total, integrated expression of our spirits, souls and bodies is in our relationships. A vital part of wholeness is what happens to us in our contact and communication with people. We are not whole as we were meant to be until we are free to develop deep, satisfying relationships with loved ones and friends. Wholeness is not a solo flight. We were made for community. Christ's indwelling in our spirits, His control of the issues of our minds is focused in the countenance of our bodies in our interfacing with people. Our faces will reflect that the King is in residence and our touch and helpful actions will mediate His gracious love.

People are to our wholeness what wings are to a bird and sails to a boat. The Lord gives us others to make us complete. Taking time for creative relationships is our expression of healthy self-love. Friends are a gift. Samuel Johnson, English lexicographer and author (1709-1784), was right. "A man, sir, should keep his friendships in constant repair." A friend is one who knows all about us and won't go away. We all need friends who affirm us, hold us to our best, lift us up when we fall, forgive us before we ask, share an adventuresome dream with us, and empathize in the valleys and mountaintops with equal sensitivity. The best way to have friends is to be one. When we ask ourselves what kind of friends we want, and dare to be that kind of person, we will have more friends than we ever imagined possible. We are not whole until we can be to people what Christ has been to us in our spirits, souls and bodies.

Wholeness, then, is the maximum development of our lives spiritually, intellectually, emotionally, volitionally, physically and relationally. It encompasses our relationships with God, self, others and our life in the world.

One last thing needs to be said. <u>Nothing debilitates wholeness more than the emphasis on one of these aspects of our nature to the neglect of the rest</u>. We all know people who are intent on one or more to the exclusion of the others. The Lord wants us to live fully in all dimensions, without imbalance or distortion.

We all know spiritual people who don't think, or intellectuals who have no concern or warmth, or dedicated people who are emotionally immature, or emotional believers who need to couple their enthusiasm with obedience, or biblical Christians who can't get along with others. None of these examples will do for us. We've been called to move on beyond any of the debilitating categories they represent. The Lord has chosen us to live life as it was meant to be. We are not "fragmatists" but unified, integrated people privileged to receive the gift of peace and experience wholeness of spirit, soul and body. The abundant life is now!

9

The Son Has Come Out

Second Thessalonians 1

*We ourselves boast of you...for your patience and
faith in all your persecutions and
tribulations that you endure.*

The musical *Annie* is a couple of hours of sheer delight
and an affirmation of life. Little Orphan Annie infuses hope
and positive expectation in everyone from Daddy Warbucks
to F.D.R. with enthusiastic singing of the theme song,
"Tomorrow." The words have lingered in my mind ever since I
had the relaxing pleasure of hearing of Annie's simple trust
that things will be different in our tomorrows.

> *The sun'll come out tomorrow*
> *Bet your bottom dollar*
> *That tomorrow there'll be sun,*
> *Just thinkin' about tomorrow*
> *Clears away the cobwebs and the sorrow*
> *Till there's none.*[9]

As I was leaving the theater with these words tumbling

about in my mind, I overheard a man say to his wife, "I sure feel better after that! Funny thing, I forgot my troubles for two solid hours. Maybe the sun will come out tomorrow for us."

Strange, isn't it, how a simple song of hope can lift people out of discouragement with life's troubles. Trouble is a universal experience. Everybody has some. No one is exempt. It comes to young and old, rich and poor, talented and inept, believers and nonbelievers, people inside and outside the church.

Will the sun really come out tomorrow? Will tomorrow be better than today? Will we get a breakthrough to new hope for our troubles? What happens when yesterday's troubles blend into today's troubles and we are left with little expectation for a different tomorrow? We say, "Annie's song was great for Broadway and Hollywood theater, but isn't that nothing more than a simplistic wish-dream?" How can we endure in our troubles when the clouds don't break open for the sun to shine through?

Mark Twain was right. "Trouble has done it. Bilgewater, trouble has done it; trouble has brung these gray hairs and this premature balditude." But it does more than that: it wears us down, takes the zest out of life and brings us to that discouraged state wherein we begin to expect trouble as the inevitable stuff of life. Some people get so used to trouble that they are uneasy without it and inadvertently do things to perpetuate its uncomfortable tension. George Herbert said, "He that seeks trouble never misses."

My definition of trouble is anything which disrupts our dreams. Big troubles are those which interrupt our life plan and purposes; little troubles are distressing fouls setting back any day's game plan. We can grapple with the latter but it's the former which wear us down. It is the diversion of the flow of life from our goals into an eddy of disappointment that gets to us.

Few of us could say that life has turned out as we planned.

Even those of us who would attest that life has developed infinitely better than we could ever have imagined would have to admit that it has not been without troubles. We've all experienced the hard discipline of desires denied and visions vanquished. But we are in good company. The spiritual giants of Scripture and the adventuresome saints of history became the frontiersmen they were because of how they handled trouble. They all knew the agitating addition of trouble to their life agendas.

We are forced to grapple with the causes of trouble. We bring a lot of it on ourselves. Poor judgment, unguided decisions, selfishness, pride and negativism all contribute to our self-made troubles. People are the second major cause of trouble. Who doesn't have his or her share of troublesome people who either stand in the way of our moving forward to our dreams and plans or who agitate the flow of our river of life with whirlpools of their personal confusion? Another cause of trouble comes in life's sicknesses, reversals, broken relationships, loss of loved ones, and fractured hopes. The closed doors of circumstances trouble all of us. But there's a deeper reason we have troubles. We are God's beloved people who must live in a fallen creation in which Satan is a persistent troublemaker for those who belong to the Lord. He can take all the other sources of trouble and use them to unsettle our confidence both in the Lord and ourselves.

The Thessalonian Christians were experiencing trouble from all of the above. Their conversion did not assure a trouble-free life. In fact, their faith in Jesus Christ was the source of most of their troubles! They now had a new set of goals, plans and purposes for their lives and circumstances. Difficult people within and without the fellowship, plus harassment of Satan, were disrupting their discipleship. Did Christ know, understand or care? Was He in the battle with them? They were forced to face the fact that life in Christ did not mean exemption from trouble, but the discovery of His power to endure in trouble. Intimacy with Christ does not assure a smooth, easy life, but an exciting companionship with Him in the battle for righteousness in a troubled world.

Paul's second letter to the Thessalonians deals directly with how to endure in trouble. That's why a careful study and exposition of its themes is so crucial today. It gives us the equipment for enduring when things don't work out as we've planned. Or when being faithful to Christ has gotten us into trouble. It presses us beyond Annie's wording. The Son, not the sun, will come out not just tomorrow but today.

We are more able to endure trouble by the sure conviction that Christ, indwelling in us, will never give us more than we can take. He will use all that happens to us for our growth and His glory. His punctual interventions will be perfectly timed so that we can praise Him and know again that He is in control and is greater than the forces of evil. The Lord's encouragement in trouble is the source of endurance through trouble!

For me, the two key words of this first chapter are "trouble" and "endurance." Paul's prayer for the Thessalonians was "that you endure" (v.4) and the Lord would "give you who are troubled rest" (v.7). After writing his customary salutation with the promise of grace and peace, Paul launches into thanksgiving and praise for the way the Thessalonians were handling trouble with Christ-inspired endurance. The flow of thought gives us an outline for our consideration of authentic endurance.

First, *trouble is the crucible in which we can grow in greatness*. It was happening to the Thessalonians. Paul's commendation expresses that. "We are bound to thank God always for you, brethren, as it is fitting, because your faith grows exceedingly, and the love of every one of you all abounds toward each other, so that we ourselves boast of you among the churches of God for your patience and faith in all your persecutions and tribulations *that you endure*" (vv. 3,4, italics added). The trouble the Thessalonians were going through was like a refining fire for raw material. It had raised the dross to the surface to be skimmed off; the pure molten metal had been centered and then poured out into the steel of girders for strong personality.

The Thessalonians' faith had become stronger as they learned to trust Christ in trouble. It had *grown exceedingly.* Paul uses a compound verb, *huperauxanei,* meaning growth above (*huper*) the expected measurements. Like Jesus' parable of the mustard seed, the faith of the Thessalonians had grown to a strong, tall tree. Their faith was not an escape from reality, but the power to live as the Lord's people in it.

Faith grows in trouble. I know that from my own life. It has made me depend on the Lord. He constantly presses me out into new challenges in which I have no visible means of support. But I have Him! In trouble I've learned to depend on the promise of two of my life verses. "Let not your heart be troubled" (John 14:1); "I am leaving you with a gift—peace of mind and heart! And the peace I give isn't fragile like the peace the world gives. So don't be troubled or afraid. Remember what I told you...I will come...to you" (John 14:27,28 TLB).

Trouble for me tests the extent to which I am living a supernatural life. I believe the world should be astounded by what the Lord does with us in trouble. In it we discover that the Lord is able. The trumpet blast of the New Testament church is that He is able. He is with us when we are tempted to give up. "He is able to aid those who are tempted" (Heb. 2:18). He is our High Priest making intercession for our strength in trouble. "He is also able to save to the uttermost those who come to God by Him, seeing He ever lives to make intercession for them" (Heb. 7:25). He will never allow trouble to defeat us. "Now to Him who is able to keep you from stumbling, and to present you faultless before the presence of His glory with exceeding joy..." (Jude 24). His power is greater than Satan's beguiling use of discouragement. "He is able even to subdue all things to Himself" (Phil. 3:21). He keeps His promise to overcome the demons of despair when we surrender our troubles to Him and are willing to grow through them. "For I know whom I have believed and am persuaded that He is able to keep what I have committed to Him until that Day" (2 Tim. 1:12). Trouble gives us an opportunity to discover the triumphant sufficiency of His power at work in us. "Now to Him who is able to do exceedingly abundantly above all that we ask or think, according to the power that works in us" (Eph. 3:20). Our hope in trouble is not that we are able, but that He is able. The Son will come out, and in, today!

For many years I lived with the erroneous assumption that a trouble-free life is a sign of the Lord's approval. I kept striving to subdue all problems so I could be free to serve Him more completely. I looked at trouble as His judgment. If I only loved Him sufficiently, I would have no troubles. I hear the same fallacious reasoning from others. "God must be punishing me or I wouldn't have problems to cope with," people often say. To be sure, some of our troubles we have brought on ourselves and others are the result of rebellion against God. These need to be confessed and healed by His grace. Once that's done we can get on the battle line to fight for truth and righteousness. If trouble comes from that, praise God! It's a sure sign that we've taken on soul-sized troubles in cooperating with Him in confronting evil in the world.

What are your troubles right now? Difficult people? Impossible circumstances? Problem situations? Conflict in relationships? Financial needs? Worry over your loved ones? The tension of growing up or growing old? World conditions? Frustration with your congregation? Focus your own particular set of troubles. Now honestly discern the cause. If you are to blame, confess that to the Lord. If other people in your life are the cause, consider what you would say or do to them if you completely trusted the One who is able. If circumstantial problems have you in a bind remember that when you trust the Lord completely, He will come to you to give you exactly what you need to be obedient to His guidance. The evidence that we have surrendered our troubles is that we can say, "Lord, thank you for allowing this trouble as an opportunity for me to grow in my faith and receive your strength to match my struggle."

The second thing Paul helps us to learn in this passage is that *trouble is an opportunity for our love for each other to be deepened.* He affirmed the growth in love which trouble had intensified in the Thessalonian church. "And the love of every one of you all abounds toward each other" (v.3). Trouble helps us to realize how much we depend on Christian friends. The syndrome of self-dependence is broken and we are able to receive from the Lord through others. Often trouble sets us free to express love we have felt but were reluctant to communicate. As a woman in my church said, "I can now thank the Lord for the troubles I have been through. I never realized how much love my fellow church members had for me." The comment about this woman by one of those helpers was revealing: "This is the first time I ever felt she needed me. She's always so put-together. This time of trouble has helped galvanize a friendship we didn't know we had." We were never meant to make it alone either without the Lord or the fellowship of concerned Christian friends. It is in trouble that deep relationships are forged. Trouble mortifies our pride and frees us to reach out. We were never meant to suffer alone. When we share our troubles we find that we are not solitary sufferers.

It is liberating to thank the Lord for troubles which prepare us to be sensitive to the troubled. G.A. Studdert Kennedy, British preacher, said that any person who is undisturbed by the pain and suffering about him is himself suffering either from hardening of the heart or softening of the brain. If we allow Him, the Lord will use everything we have been or are going through to equip us to be loving enablers.

We can share with others what happens in troubles when the Lord intervenes.

That leads us to the third truth about trouble which Paul teaches us through what He wrote to the Thessalonians. Trouble not only strengthens our faith and puts us into love's service for others, *it gives us an opportunity to receive the gift of endurance*. Paul was proud of the endurance of the Thessalonians. "We ourselves boast of you among the churches of God for your patience and faith in all your persecutions and tribulations that you endure" (v.4). Faith multiplied by trouble and divided by the Lord's interventions, equals endurance.

Authentic endurance is not white-knuckled, teeth-gritting determination to survive in trouble. It is rooted in the confidence that the Lord will invade the trouble at just the right time with His unlimited resources. He knows, cares and will intervene. Troubles are an opportunity to experience the power of the Lord in a fresh way. We can say with the psalmist, "This poor man cried and the Lord heard him; and saved him out of all his troubles" (Ps. 34:6). "God is our refuge and strength, a very present help in trouble" (Ps. 46:1). Endurance grows out of the realization that the Lord will come to us in the midnight darkness of trouble. He comes not only to comfort but to perform miracles we could never have imagined. He has resources to unleash we had not counted on. He can untangle knotty problems, change the attitudes of troublesome people, give us wisdom beyond our understanding, and open closed doors.

Paul reminds the Thessalonians that endurance is not the result of wishful thinking but of confidence in the Lord Jesus. The apostle reminds them of a central theme of his first letter: Christ came, comes and is coming. Endurance is based on what Christ did on Calvary, comes to do in each of our troubles, and will come as the ultimate judge of history. All troubles must be seen in the light of that threefold assurance. With that antidote for trouble we can second Phillips

Brooks's resolution: "Do not pray for easy lives. Pray to be stronger men. Do not pray for tasks equal to your powers. Pray for powers equal to your tasks!"[10] That power comes from the intervening Lord.

The very week in which I am writing this chapter has been a personal time of growth in endurance. I began the week with worries about the finances for my church's television ministry. Launching this outreach mission has forced me to trust the Lord completely. Monday was a troublesome day of surrendering the project again. On Tuesday I had lunch with a faithful giver to the program. He told me that he had had the television ministry on his heart. He had prayed, "Lord, if this venture is your will for us, give me a sign." He was led to put out a fleece by placing a condominium he owned on the market, with the promise to the Lord that he would give the profit to the television fund. The substantial amount the Lord put in his mind was exactly what was needed to proceed with further production. The gift would be dependent on the sale of the property at the price the man was led to establish for the property. If he were to sell it for less, the profit would be less than what we needed. Because of the tight money market and the high interest rates for mortgages, a quick sale seemed unlikely.

We paused over lunch to pray. The Lord knew our need not only for the full amount but for a renewed sign of His affirmation of the ministry. We surrendered the whole trouble to Him.

The very next day a buyer purchased the property for cash! We should not have been surprised. The Lord knew the urgency. Three wonderful things resulted from the miracle. First, the Lord used the intervention to assure me that the television ministry was indeed His will for me and the church. The fleece was wringing wet! Second, the exact amount needed taught us again that the Lord knows our need and delights to astound us with His timeliness. Third, endurance was imbued. If He loved us that much in this need, we could trust Him with all our troubles! Now at the end of the week, I'm engrossed in new challenges and am tackling them with the fresh gusto of this week's miracle.

God gives us those special assurances to strengthen the muscle of our endurance. Outward trouble is to the Christian what tempests are to the oak tree. They serve to make the roots stronger. Trouble can temporarily rob us of tranquility or a smooth, easy life, but the one thing they can't take from us is our right to choose what our attitude will be. I am convinced that the true need of our hearts is the heart of our needs. And Christ satisfies that need with the gift of endurance. In trouble we move from the world's idea of peace to the peace of Christ. "Therefore, having been justified by faith, we have peace with God through our Lord Jesus Christ, through whom also we have access by faith into this grace in which we stand, and rejoice in hope of the glory of God. And not only that, but we also glory in tribulations, knowing that tribulation produces perseverance; and perseverance, character; and character, hope. And hope does not disappoint, because the love of God has been poured out in our hearts by the Holy Spirit who was given to us" (Rom. 5:1-5).

Any trouble is worth it if in our struggle we are brought into that quality of peace. Troubles break the syndrome of independence and willfulness and bring us back to our Lord. Luther said that he who has not tasted the bitter cannot savor the sweet.

There's a remarkable verse in 2 Chronicles 29:27 which describes what happens when we surrender our troubles. Hezekiah had restored worship in the Temple after the apostasy of Ahaz's reign. "When the burnt offering began, the song to the Lord also began with the trumpets." Our troubles are our burnt offering. When they are placed on the altar, the song of the Lord and the trumpets of freedom begin. Endurance for the future is the fruit of burnt offerings of trouble on the altar of relinquishment today.

Henry van Dyke must have made a burnt offering of his trouble before he wrote the poem about how to find peace in trouble.

With eager heart and will on fire
I sought to win my great desire.
"Peace shall be mine," I said, but life
Grew bitter in the endless strife.

My soul was weary, and my pride
Was wounded deep. To heaven I cried,
"God give me peace, or I must die."
The dumb stars glittered no reply.

Broken at last I bowed my head
Forgetting all myself and said:
"Whatever comes, His will be done."
And in that moment peace was won."[11]

Any trouble that brings us to that sublime experience is worth the price of admission. At that moment of trust, endurance that lasts is given. Look, the Son has come out!

10

Our Gospel

Second Thessalonians 2

*He called you by our gospel, for the obtaining of
the glory of our Lord Jesus Christ.*

I stood outside an auditorium waiting to be introduced to
preach. An outstanding, elderly, evangelical scholar, whom I
respect very much, came up to me with a moving challenge.
"Give us the gospel according to Lloyd!"

I must have shown shock on my face at this startling
admonition. The brilliant, seasoned saint went on to explain: "We want to hear what Christ means to you; the difference He has made in your life; the way the biblical truth is
enabling you to cope with the tough issues today. Give us the
distilled essence of your gospel passed through the fires of
experience."

As I waited, reflecting on that, my mind drifted back to
some favorite words spoken long ago by Bishop William
Alfred Quayle, the American Methodist bishop (1860-1925).
They are equally applicable to the witness of the laity or
clergy. "Preaching is the art of making a sermon and delivering that. Why no, that is not preaching. Preaching is the art
of making a preacher, and delivering that. Preaching is the

outrush of soul in speech. Therefore the elemental business in preaching is not with the preaching but with the preacher. It is no trouble to preach, but a vast trouble to construct a preacher. What, then, in the light of this is the task of a preacher? [Or of anyone sharing his or her faith.] Mainly this, the amassing of a great soul so as to have something worthwhile to give—the sermon is the preacher up to date."[12]

This chapter deals with our gospel up to date. A gospel that assures us not only of what Christ has done for us but also includes all dimensions of time and eternity. If we are to survive in trouble as we considered it in the previous chapter, it will require a gospel which is personally and passionately ours.

The word "gospel" means good news. The word in Greek, *euaggelion,* had three uses in ancient times: It meant the bearer of good news, the good news itself, and the reward given to the bearer of the good news. All three have meaning for us. We are the communicators of the good news of the life, message, death, reconciliation and resurrection of Jesus Christ. What He accomplished for our salvation, eternal life and abundant living is the content of our good news. He, Himself, is our reward.

The gospel contains the truth of what Christ did and does. It is the declaration of the promise of life as it was meant to be. The content of the gospel is the message of the New Testament. It is to become my gospel and your gospel. The gospel according to you and me is the gospel which has been ingrained into our thinking, understanding, action and attitude. Biblical truth passed through the tempering of experience until it is an integrated part of us. We are not only to believe the good news, but are to be good news incarnate. The gospel on two legs walking. Only "our" gospel can sustain us in a time like this.

Paul would agree. In 2 Thessalonians 2:14, he speaks of "our gospel." He meant the message of salvation, sanctification and glorification he had communicated to the Thessalonians. His good news contained the exciting message of the three advents we talked about earlier. Many of the problems that were being faced by the Thessalonians were the result of the fact that they had not made Paul's gospel their gospel. The great need in the Thessalonian church was for understanding and conviction about the events of the end times. Paul's second letter to them was to make one more attempt to straighten out their thinking.

"Therefore, brethren, stand fast and hold the traditions which you have been taught, whether by word or our epistle" (v. 15). The word "tradition" means that which has been handed down to us, which we make our own. Paul was calling for traditional Christians, people whose lives were firmly rooted in undeniable truth. He did not mean rites, rules and regulations. Nor did he imply customs or practices. What he did mean was the essential truth he had preached and written about the Lord who came, comes and is coming.

Our gospel is the compounded truth of Christ and the Scriptures for all of life. So many of the frustrating questions we grapple with, and the complex uncertainties about life that cripple us, are the result of not having our own gospel. The new church which is being born in our time will be made up of people who can boldly say "according to my gospel . . . !"

This second chapter of 2 Thessalonians is one that I find easier to interpret by starting at the end and then going back to the beginning. The concluding verses give a context of what Paul wrote in the first 12 verses of the chapter. He wanted the Thessalonians to be established on the firm foundation of the truth of the gospel which would give them "everlasting consolation and good hope by grace" (v. 16) for their hearts.

My prayer is that what Paul had to reteach will become a solid part of our gospel—yours and mine. Since many of us share the same uncertainties that the Thessalonians experienced, we need the same "traditions" incorporated into our gospel so we can be assured personally and be able to communicate clarity and hope to others. The Master's command has not gone out of style: "Go into all the world and preach the gospel to every creature" (Mark 16:15). And Paul's urgency must be ours. "Necessity is laid upon me; yes, woe is me if I do not preach the gospel!" (1 Cor. 9:16). Throughout his letters, the apostle speaks of the truth of the gospel, the faith of the gospel, the joy of the gospel, being worthy of the gospel, the glorious gospel and the advance of the gospel.

Now in this section of 2 Thessalonians, Paul wants his beloved friends to include in their gospel much clearer thinking about a problem he had addressed earlier. We are comforted by the fact that he had to go over basics again. They didn't hear and learn any better than we do. The old problem of confusion over the end times had persisted. False teachers within and from without the church still were purveying fallacious facsimiles of Paul's original teaching. Truth had been twisted again. Note the apostle's patience as he takes them back over the essentials. A good example for those of us who think that just because something is said or written, it is understood. Paul really loved these people!

The spirit and content of this chapter of 2 Thessalonians reveals three crucial things which can happen to us when the gospel becomes our gospel.

First of all, *a gospel which is ours will free us from being shaken in mind or troubled. The Living Bible* paraphrase of verses 1-3 clarifies the situation in Thessalonica. "And now, what about the coming again of our Lord Jesus Christ, and our being gathered together to meet Him? Please don't be upset and excited, dear brothers, by the rumor that this day of the Lord has already begun. If you hear of people having visions and special messages from God about this, or letters that are supposed to have come from me, don't believe them. Don't be carried away and deceived regardless of what they say." The word for "troubled" or "upset" means being tossed to and fro by the waves of a storm. Only clear thinking about the gospel can help us steer a straight course through the turbulent waters of false opinions, theories and esoteric visions of others. When truth becomes our character, we are able to withstand the changing currents of thought which swirl around us.

The Thessalonian church was a hotbed of questions and confused answers about the progression of the rapture, tribulation and millennium. The new focus of the old problem which occasioned this letter from Paul was that some were teaching that if the glorious coming of the Lord to call believers to Himself was to be followed by the tribulation, and the church was undergoing persecution, then surely Christ had come and they had missed His coming. Just as concern about those who had died before Christ's return prompted Paul's message in 1 Thessalonians 4, so too this troublesome new teaching motivated the apostle to write again. "Calm down!" he seems to be saying. "Get back to basics, the traditions I taught you. According to the gospel I gave you the end will not come until there is this kind of trouble. Don't be confused, the problems you are having are nothing in comparison with the anguish which unbelievers will experience during the tribulation."

The crucial thing about this for us is that when the biblical truth becomes our gospel, we can discern false teaching and not be thrown into turmoil by it. We live in a period of history which makes the Thessalonian problems easy by comparison. False prophets of both hope and doom are gathering large followings around untruth. Cults, sects, non-biblical preaching, as well as movements to bring personal utopia on earth, are everywhere. Add to that the watered-down, self-indulgent facsimiles of the biblical truth in many churches, and you have a time in which profound communion with the Lord and clear thinking guided by His Spirit are absolutely required. When the gospel is ours, we can withstand the heresies. Paul reminds us that the "falling away comes first" before the Lord returns, "and the man of sin is revealed, the son of perdition" (2:3). The church will be strengthened by the defection of the uncommitted. There will be a parade of false movements which pretend to be the church.

This has practical application today. Think of Rev. Moon's Unification Church or the Church of Scientology, to name two out of hundreds of groups misusing the name of church and parading doctrines of salvation, rebirth, faith and fulfillment which are blatantly non-biblical. Or consider the wildfire growth of psychic groups or psychological self-help "fellowships" which are a substitute for Christ for a growing number of people. Our gospel must give us clarity about these distortions and keep our ship on course. There is more in our time to indicate the "falling away" before the end than the Thessalonians could have imagined.

The Greek word for "falling away" is *apostasia* from which our word "apostasy" is taken. It was originally a military term for defection or political rebellion. So often apostasy begins with a confusion of loyalties. And that is rooted in self-will multiplied by fuzzy thinking. The problem has been around a long time—since Adam and Eve. But Paul's gospel incorporated an understanding of that. And so should ours. We need not be alarmed. The Lord told us it would happen. There will be false prophets, pseudo-christs, self-indulgent leaders to lead others astray. Jonestown is a ghastly reminder that we should not be surprised by "falling away."

The second thing that a gospel which is ours will give us is *power to understand and confront evil*. Paul's teaching here reiterates what we need to claim as our own truth. The apostle took Satan and evil seriously. In this passage his thinking is undergirded with four basic assumptions: (1) there is an abject power of evil in the world, named Satan, in deadly conflict with God; (2) the human heart is the battlefield on which this combat is waged; (3) when we accept Jesus Christ as Lord and Saviour, we are sealed against

Satan's possession or dominance; and (4) the name of Jesus is our all-powerful weapon to defeat Satan's evil power.

Based on the preceding presuppositions we can contemplate what Paul says about the temptation of the Thessalonians to entertain the assumption that Satan was winning. To offset that, Paul says that the "falling away" is only a sign of the approaching time of the Lord's return. This would be coupled with a rise to power of our evil leader who will be the human incarnation of the power of Satan. Scripture calls him the Antichrist. John refers to him extensively in his letters to the churches in Asia Minor. He uses the term for the historical figure who will arise, for the Gnostics who denied that Christ lived in the flesh, and for believers who had defected the fellowship of the church. The word "antichrist" is an interesting combination of the preposition *anti* and the word *christos. Anti* means either opposition or substitution. The historical figure Paul describes will be both. His opposition will be in his substitution for Christ, his claim to be a surrogate messiah.

In verse 4 of 2 Thessalonians 2, Paul describes him, the son of perdition, as a beguiling leader who will exalt himself above God and claim to be God in history. This incarnate Satan will reign just prior to the rapture and the tribulation. It was not the responsibility of the Thessalonians, or us, to single out any despot of history as *the* Antichrist, which is tempting in any age. Evil monarchs, corrupt popes, ravaging generals of various periods have earned the designation. But they have been folded into the pages of history and the real rapture and tribulation have not come. Perhaps we had better stop prognosticating and get on with the promulgation of our gospel. Jesus said plainly that the end would not come until the good news was preached to all nations.

The important thing to remember from Paul's teaching to the Thessalonians in this challenging, difficult chapter is that God is Lord over history. He is not vanquished by Satan, nor will He be subdued by the Antichrist, whoever he will be and whenever he will rise to power as the portent of the end.

Move on now to savor the assurance of verses 6 and 7. Before the time of his reign, the son of perdition is being restrained. "And now you know what is restraining, that he may be revealed in his own time. For the mystery of lawlessness is already at work; only He who now restrains will do so until He is taken out of the way." I am pleased that *The New King James Bible* capitalizes one of the pronouns of these verses to help us grasp the awesome truth Paul is communicating as a tradition for our gospel. Who is restraining Satan in our age except the Holy Spirit? We are sealed against satanic possession. He may hassle and even influence a Christian but his powers are limited by the protecting ministry of the Holy Spirit. Don't leave that out of your gospel! The evil one is constantly working to unsettle believers and disrupt the church. But the name of Jesus is more powerful than Satan's crafty strategies. Whenever we claim the name of Jesus, we can defeat his influence. When we are disturbed personally by his debilitating tactics or when the fellowship of the church is undermined, we should rebuke Satan in Christ's name. That calls in the restrainer, the Holy Spirit, the living, present Christ Himself. Here's a good formula: "Satan, you have no power over me; I charge you in the name of Christ Jesus to get your hands off me and the people I love. You are a deceiver. Christ won the battle with you on Calvary. Now get out of my life!"

I will never forget a summer in which my wife and I were under attack. Early in July I left with my two sons to lead a Holy Land tour. One night in a hotel room in Jerusalem I awoke pinned to the bed. I could not move. A gigantic force held me immobilized. When I was fully awake, any efforts to move were subdued. At first, I thought I was physically paralyzed, but each time I tried to raise a part of my body, I was slapped back as if glued to the bed. In the darkness it suddenly dawned on me what was happening. I cried out in a shout, "In the name of Jesus, Satan unpin me and leave this room. I belong to Jesus of Nazareth, the Saviour of the world, Messiah and Lord of all! Now leave me alone." Immediately I was released and a powerful peace flowed into my heart and surrounded me. The darkness of the room was turned into a brightness and then faded into darkness again. The Restrainer had come. The Holy Spirit!

The remarkable thing about this bizarre event was that it occurred on the same night my wife was grappling with the distressing news that she had cancer and would have to undergo extensive surgery and treatment. But now five years later, I am pleased to report that she is completely cured. Neither one of us can ever doubt either the attack of Satan or the triumph of Jesus Christ over him. But it has helped us to feel as well as think through what it might have been like not to have the restraining power of the Lord protecting us. It was a personal intimation of what the tribulation will be like for unbelievers when the Restrainer is removed and Satan has full control of the world. Ghastly!

I do not want to paint myself into a simplistic corner. Sickness is not always a satanic attack nor is death a sign of God's judgment. I know too many people who have claimed the name of Jesus for healing for whom recovery was not a part of God's specific plan. But I have seen Satan's demons of despair restrained and the Holy Spirit's comfort and joy sustain people. Death is not an ending for us who belong to Christ and the excruciating anguish is removed by the divine Restrainer.

This leads to the third "tradition" Paul passes on for inclusion in our gospel. The Restrainer, the Holy Spirit, is also the Revealer. *He will expose Satan so that the Christians can see him for what he is*. The final victory of the battle between the Lord and Satan is sure. I believe that Paul is talking about the triumph over Satan that will take place at the end of the seven-year tribulation. "And then the lawless one will be revealed, whom the Lord will consume with the breath of His mouth and destroy with the brightness of

His coming" (v. 8). The diminutive triumphs we can have over Satan by calling on the name of Jesus are only a foretaste of his final demise. We can be sure that God will have the final word!

What follows in Paul's teaching in verses 8 to 12 is a description of conditions during the tribulation. Satan and unbelievers will have unlimited control of the earth. The righteous influence of the church will be removed. Those who have resisted Christ or refused to believe in Him as Saviour and Lord will be left behind. They will believe in the antichrist as a savior but will be the deluded sufferers of a world without love, peace, forgiveness and beauty. The final judgment will only climax the judgment in which they have been forced to live in the tribulation.

After digesting this awesome truth, we are more than ready to return to the place where we began this chapter. Paul's transitional "but" is most welcome like the first rays of the sun after a long night. We have been forced to grapple with aspects of the gospel we neglect or overlook. We've had a taste of hell on earth and are ready to burst into a doxology as we count ourselves among the saints. *But,* indeed! "But we are bound to give thanks to God always for you, brethren beloved by the Lord, because God has from the beginning chosen you for salvation through sanctification by the Spirit and belief in the truth" (v. 13). We are the called and chosen, beloved and cherished, loved and forgiven people of God! We belong to Him and that will never change. The troubles we experience are not a sign that we are left in the tribulation but an opportunity to receive the power of the Restrainer, Liberator and Protector of our souls. Heaven has begun for us in the sublime companionship of the Lord. All the next stage of our eternal life can be is better. Indescribably better!

Now we can pray: "Lord God of all creation, we praise you that you know the beginning and the end. Thank you for raising up a new church in our time, and for including us in your eternal family. Help us to trust you in difficult times and leave the results to you. May the distortions of the gospel around us strengthen rather than weaken the development of our Christ-centered, biblically-rooted gospel. Give us the sure confidence that frees us from being shaken in mind or troubled in spirit.

"As we have considered aspects of the gospel dealing with your judgment and triumph over evil, we have been brought to a new depth of praise and gratitude that we belong to you. Thank you, Lord, for choosing us, calling us, giving us the gift of faith to accept our salvation through Jesus Christ our Lord, and for making us whole through your sanctifying work in us. We trust you completely with our daily lives. Seal us against Satan's attack and guard us with your shielding grace from any subtle influence he may try to use on us. We want to live our days for you without reservation. If the end of history as we know it comes in our lifetime, we thank you in advance that we shall share in Christ's glory and rejoice in His victory. Now we commit ourselves to live the good news. Thank you for *our* gospel, our assurance and hope for all time and eternity. In the name of Jesus through whom you have made it all possible. Hallelujah and Amen!"

11

"It's Winnin' Time!"

Second Thessalonians 3:1-5

*Finally, brethren, pray for us, that the word of the
Lord may have free course and be glorified,
just as with you.*

I have spent the 32 years of my life in Christ seeking to be
a free person. I long to be free to love, forgive, respond to life
spontaneously, expect miracles and live as a celebrant of life.
My experience of Christ's love constantly frees me from self-
justification and guilt. His grace has liberated me to trust
Him with my problems and needs. Countless interventions
have convinced me that He knows my needs and will answer
prayer beyond my fondest imagination. Times of self-doubt
have been replaced by a deep inner peace. And yet, I have felt
that I have only begun to experience what it means to be free.

When we talk of Christian freedom, we usually mean
what Christ does to set us free to live the abundant life. Now I
suspect that is only the beginning of authentic freedom. I feel
I've been on the edge of this deeper discovery of real freedom
for a long time. The Lord has been preparing me to move on
to something more. I have found it here in the third chapter
of 2 Thessalonians. It's no secret; it has been there for cen-

turies. I don't know how I missed it reading this passage hundreds of times through the years. But then, the Lord's timing is perfect. The Holy Spirit has waited until I was ready. Perhaps you know about this secret already and will smile as I pour out in words the excitement of my discovery. If so, rejoice with me and reaffirm your own experience of the truth. If not, join me in uncovering the treasure.

When Paul asked the Thessalonians to pray for him and his missionary friends, Timothy and Silas, he did not ask that they be set free to serve Christ, but that they would give Christ freedom to work in and through them. Look at this amazing prayer request: "Finally, brethren, pray for us, that the word of the Lord may have free course and be glorified, just as with you" (3:1). With a ravenous hunger for new truth, I checked my Greek New Testament. Paul used a metaphor from the Greek games for running a race. An apt paraphrase would be: "May the word of the Lord have a glorified run in us!" The present subjunctive is used: may He keep on running and being glorified. The two verbs *trechēi* and *doxazētai* are not used together anywhere else in the New Testament. Lightfoot translates the phrase, "may He have a triumphant career." The apostle's request is for prayer that Christ might win His race through him. The concern is not just for freedom to run the race of discipleship for the Lord, but to allow the Lord to run in and through him without reservations or obstructions.

Paul often used the metaphor of running a race to explain the Christian life, but usually to illustrate his race for Christ. In 1 Corinthians 9:24-27 he talks about running the race to win the imperishable crown. Galatians 2:2 refers to his apostolic calling as a race which he confirmed with the church leaders in Jerusalem. Again in Romans 9:16 the believer is described by the athletic term of runner. Philippians 2:16 expresses Paul's desire to hold fast the word of life so that he will not have run in vain. Second Timothy 4:7 is vividly autobiographical near the end of the apostle's life. "I have fought the good fight, I have finished the race, I have kept the faith." The longing to run for the Lord with freedom from any encumbrance is also expressed in Hebrews 12:1. "Therefore, seeing we also are surrounded by so great a cloud of witnesses, let us lay aside every weight, and the sin which so easily ensnares us, and let us run with endurance the race that is set before us."

A friend of mine who lived an adventuresome life caught the enthusiasm of Paul in living for Christ. "Lloyd," he said, just before he died, "it's been a good run. I'm going to receive my crown. See you in heaven!"

But here is Paul in our text going beyond even that lovely imagery. He shifts metaphors and now it is the Lord who is pictured as running the race through us. "Keep on praying for us," the giant among the greatest men of history pleaded, "that the word of the Lord may run its race and receive its crown of glory." The Word of the Lord was not just the conceptualized message of the Lord that Paul was commissioned to preach, but a synonym for the presence of the Lord. It implies that intimate union with Christ from which Paul received power and guidance, motive and will. When he longed for the Word to dwell richly in his friends at Colossae (see Col. 3:16), he prayed for nothing less than Christ's indwelling presence.

Christ is the Word of God, the eternal Logos, the creative and recreative verb of the Lord. Twenty-two times in the Gospel of John, the Lord said, "I am," *egō eimi,* in self-declaration of being God with us. The same infinitive is used for "I am who I am" in the Greek translation of the Hebrew in the Exodus account of the burning bush. Yahweh who appeared to Moses, came in Jesus Christ. And Paul wanted Christ to have complete freedom to run His race in him with free course and glory.

The Lord frees us so we can give Him freedom. Authentic freedom is clearing the track, opening the way, removing the impediments, letting go with joyous abandonment.

Most of us have spent enough time and energy imagining what it would mean to be free people. There's a new, gigantic leap to freeedom to be taken. It is to imagine all the facets of our nature, all the relationships of our lives, all the possibilities of the future—completely open for the glorious freedom of Christ to do what He wills with us. We are amazed by the power of will He has entrusted to us. He will not invade our affairs without an invitation. We can litter the racetrack with the blocks of willful resistance. The capacity to say yes or no has been entrusted to us. To say yes is to give the Lord freedom to do His work through our lives.

The question of authentic freedom is not what can the Lord do to set us free, but what can we do to free up our lives for Him. That question forces us to wonder where in our lives we are tripping His glorious race. What areas have we kept back; what relationships of our lives are closed to Him?

The Christian life begins when we are released from the prisons of our own making. The love of the cross unlocks the prison doors of memory. The past is forgiven and the future is open to new possiblities. We are liberated to accept and love ourselves as loved by the Lord. This unshackles our relationships. We become natural, affirming people who care. Life loses its drudgery. Motivated by love, we want to serve the Lord.

All this is in preparation for the sublime freedom for which we were created. Now we are confronted with a new purpose for living. It's one stage of growth to say with Paul, "For to me to live is Christ" and quite another to say "Christ in me, the hope of glory." Christ does not ask, "What have you done for me lately," but "What will you allow me to do in and through you today?" Our challenge is not to work harder for the Lord, but to give Him freedom to work.

All we can offer the Lord is our willingness. "Lord, make me willing to be made willing! Heal my fears, unleash my timidity, unloose my clutching control." That prayer is the key to authentic freedom.

We all have areas of our life which need to be opened up for the Lord's free and glorious run. Paul had his. In the second verse of this third chapter he goes on to include in his prayer request "that we may be delivered from unreasonable and wicked men; for not all have faith." Resistance met the apostle in each of the cities where Paul preached. His experience in Corinth was no exception. But don't miss the deeper freedom here. There's a difference between asking for strength to persevere in the face of opposing obstacles or people, and surrendering them with the knowledge that the Lord can change people and unbind circumstances. In point of fact, Christ did transform the situation in Corinth. When Gallio became proconsul in the region of Achaia, the Lord reversed the currents of criticism against the apostle. The midnight vision of the Lord and His reassuring words to Paul not to be afraid had enabled the frightened missionary to trust Him with his life in Corinth. The Lord had resources in people He was ready to use. Who but the Lord could have made a Roman proconsul an ally of the cause of Christianity? In Paul's trial by the Jews before Gallio, the proconsul finally threw the case out of court and drove the accusers out defeated. In it all, Christ was running His race!

That prompts us to think about problem areas in our lives which need the power of Christ. Give Him freedom to work. Expect a breakthrough! Tell the Lord all about whatever it is that's debilitating. His gracious command is "Give that to me, let go of it, let me run with it!" Now feel the release of tension and the peace which surges into our hearts. That's freedom.

Paul goes on in verses 3, 4, and 5 to give us the basis of this new freedom. He reminds us that the Lord is faithful. The deeper level of freedom I'm discovering is firmly rooted in His faithfulness. He is Lord of all creation, all power in heaven and earth is His, He is able to do what we have decided is impossible or improbable. The more we focus on His faithfulness, the more faith-filled we become. Instead of focusing on the problematical circumstances, we are to lift our attention to His essential nature of faithfulness. He gives us freedom to choose worry or willingness, discouragement or dependence, reservation or release. The Lord's faithfulness begets the gift of faith to relinquish our lives to Him. Each evidence of His power to reign gloriously through our circumstances increases our capacity of faith in new impossibilities.

This gives us confidence. Paul says in verse 4: "And we have confidence in the Lord." The Greek word he used here for "confidence" is *pepoithamen*, meaning to persuade. Its use in this instance implies that he was in a state of being persuaded. The faithfulness of the Lord was persuading Paul to trust not only the antagonists in Corinth to the Lord but also his concern over the spiritual welfare of the Thessalonians. The Lord's run among Paul's friends was going to be a success. The things Paul had been led to command them, they would be willing to do. The church in Thessalonica belonged to the Lord, not Paul. All the apostle was asked to do was pray, releasing the church's future to the Lord.

It is amazing how we hang on to furtive fear in our work for the Lord. We forget that our challenges have been entrusted to us by Him in the first place. But we trudge along, carrying the heavy burdens expecting the Lord's approbation for what we are sacrificing of ourselves in energy and anxiety for His causes and people. What the Lord entrusts for us to do He will enable. We were never meant to do the Lord's work on our strength alone. Our challenge is to join Him in what He is doing and work with the delight of seeing the Master Craftsman create what we could never accomplish.

Such action engenders patience. Paul could let go of worry because he knew that the Lord would finish what He had begun in Thessalonica. He wanted nothing less than this same patience for his friends. "And may the Lord direct your hearts into the love of God and into the patience of Christ" (v. 5). The deeper we go into the heart of God the more patience we have to leave what we have committed up to His timing. We lose our freedom when we take back what we have relinquished in prayer.

Patience is a fruit of the Spirit, a part of the new character implant in those who give Christ free course in their lives. Here again, it is not something we conjure up for the Lord while we wait for Him to finish the race in some area we've committed to Him. Rather, patience *is* Christ in us. It is not a gift He gives, but the gift He is. His voice within us says, "Beloved, you have asked me to run with freedom in this situation. I can't do it if you put up the barriers of your willful worry. If I could accomplish your atonement on the cross and rise from the dead and return to be in you, is it too much to expect that I can do this?" Then, His patience replaces our perturbance.

Note that Paul's freedom did not come in trusting the Lord with his petty needs, but from power in the great enterprise of communicating the gospel. Authentic freedom is given to us for our partnership with the Lord in the business of the Kingdom. He is going to get His work done with or without us. If we resist Him, He will move on to others who are willing to cooperate. That leaves questions to be answered. Is what we are asking an extension of His will? If it were done would it advance His cause? Would it liberate us for greater obedience in our discipleship?

The Lord never gives us anything that will encumber us in joining the race with Him. But be sure of this: we can pray for "free course" in anything which will move forward the calling He has given us. The deepest longing of our hearts will be that the Lord will have complete freedom to do His will in, around and through us. Our part of the bargain is to be cooperative. Would you describe yourself as one with a cooperative spirit? Does He have access to all of you? Do you resist His direction at any turn? Are you completely open to what He has to say and what He may want you to do? Can you make your daily commitment, "Today I will cooperate with the Lord in all of life"?

I recently asked a man this last question. He was not a free person. His conscientious nature made it difficult to relax and believe that the Lord was at work in his problems. He asked me something you may be wondering about at this point of examination of authentic freedom. "Do you mean that I don't have to do anything? Where does hard work fit in with this quality of freedom?"

Paul is ahead of us. In verses 6 through 15 he deals with a thorny problem in the Thessalonian church. There were some of the Thessalonian Christians who used their freedom in Christ for irresponsibility. They became a burden on the fellowship, expecting to be fed and supported by loving, Christian friends. Paul warns against this idleness. He tells them bluntly, "Get to work; carry your own weight; don't use your idleness as a busybody." Using the example of his own life with them, he reminds the new Christians that he worked for a living while he was with them. Freedom does not spell irresponsibility. It means that we can work industriously but not frantically. There is dignity in work for a Christian. We all need to invest our lives in some rewarding work, but always giving glory to the Lord for the intellect, strength and will to do it. Paul sternly admonished against the "leave-it-to-the-Lord-others-will-take-care-of-me" heresy being practiced by some in Thessalonica.

The problem with most of us, however, is not idleness, but making an idol of our work. We try to find life's meaning in our work rather than bringing the meaning to our work. Success, recognition and advancement become the basis of our self-worth and esteem. There's nothing wrong with success unless it becomes so crucial that it blocks out our real reason for being.

The other day I overheard a man ask another the familiar question, "What do you do for a living?" The man's answer was a classic: "I follow Christ for my living and practice dentistry as an expression of my faith!"

Paul would have cheered that. He worked for his own support but lived for Christ. The Thessalonians were to do nothing less. And their example, like his to them, would be a challenge to those who were idle busybodies.

The thrust of this passage is that our faith in Christ makes for industrious responsibility. We are to work knowing Christ is at work. We experience freedom in our discipleship when we dare great things for the Lord, expecting great things to be done by the Lord.

Paul's benediction at the close of this second letter is a pointed conclusion. "May the Lord of peace Himself give you peace always in every way. The Lord be with you all" (v. 16). Peace from the Lord is the result of the deeper freedom we've been talking about. When we experience peace through the gift of the cross, we have the secret of trusting Christ's power in our lives. A lasting peace is inseparably related to giving Christ a "free course" in our lives. A surrendered, expectant, cooperative person in whom Christ is running His race will know profound peace.

There is no more hopeful blessing we can give or claim than "the Lord be with you." Do we believe it? The omnipresent Lord is our freedom. There is no place we can go where He will not be with us; no problem we can face for which His power will be inadequate; no person we will deal with in whom He has not been working; no situation where He has not preceded us and will show the way. Paul assures us of an awesome blessing. If we accept the blessing, we will never be alone. The Lord will live His life in us and His run will be glorious. Christ Himself is our freedom.

Consider what would happen in a congregation if it became a fellowship of this quality of authentic freedom! What if clergy, officers and members gave the Lord freedom in all the affairs of the church's life, prayers, mission and evangelism? The new church the Lord is calling in this decade is meant to be a supernatural church. One in which there is no possible explanation of transformed lives, growth, dynamic movement and outreach—except that the Lord Himself is present, unleashing His power and performing miracles.

Every congregation has its own set of problems and challenges. These are opportunities to give the Lord freedom, a free course to run. We get bogged down in our own efforts to solve problems for the Lord. He waits, withholding His blessing until we pray releasing those needs to Him. That happened to me recently. I was praying about a challenge our church in Hollywood was confronting. The only answer I seemed to get was, "I will not pour out my power until all my people pray." I shared this alarming answer with my elders. They called the whole congregation to prayer. That was the turning point. The Lord lifted the burden and ran with it for us.

Recently at a retreat, our elders committed themselves to a "Dare It Now!" year. We have long- and short-range goals the Lord has given us in prolonged times of prayerful planning. Each goal has its own challenges which make us wonder how we can reach it. The thing we are learning is that when we anticipate great things from the Lord we can dare great things with the Lord. Again and again, we are brought back to the necessity of giving Him the freedom to do the impossible. Our temptation is to do our best with our sagacity and skill. When that is inadequate we are broken and ready to let the Lord do in and through the church what we could never do for Him on a human level. The Lord wants to empower churches to astound the world. When people ask, "How did you do it?" the only answer should be, "We didn't do it. The Lord did!" There is no limit to the blessings He will give, the problems He will solve, the miracles He will perform in a congregation that will trust Him completely and give Him the glory.

Magic Johnson, the young rookie of the Los Angeles Lakers basketball team, has given us a motto for this time of unprecedented blessing of the Lord on the church. The odds were against the Los Angeles team when they played the Philadelphia 76ers for the championship. Kareem Abdul Jabbar, the star scorer of the team, was laid up with a sprained ankle and Philadelphia was slated to win by a wide margin. But Magic Johnson spurred the Lakers on to a spectacular victory with his favorite saying: "It's winnin' time!"

It *is* winnin' time for you and me . . . and the church. All because Christ is running the race for us. He has won and will win. Be sure of that! Say it in your soul and then live it with authentic freedom with all your impossibilities released to Christ. It is the *Lord's* winnin' time!

Notes

1. Lloyd John Ogilvie, *The Radiance of the Inner Splendor* (Nashville: The Upper Room, 1980).

2. Horatius Bonar (no other information available).

3. Nellie Jean Stratton (no other information available).

4. Dora Greenwell, *Living Quotations for Christians*, ed. by Sherwood E. Wirt and Kerster Beckstrom (New York: Harper & Row, 1974), p. 182.

5. William Barclay, *The Letters to the Philippians, Colossians, and Thessalonians*, The Daily Study Bible (Edinburgh: Saint Andrew Press, 1951), p. 231.

6. James Stewart, *The Wind of the Spirit* (Nashville: Abingdon Press, 1968), p. 116.

7. *"Seven Steps to Stagnation"* (Chicago: Robert H. Franke Assoc.).

8. Quoted by Harry Emerson Fosdick, *The Three Meanings—Prayer* (Chicago: Association Press; Follett Publishing Co.), p. 114.

9. TOMORROW fr. "Annie" lyric: Martin Charnin; music: Charles Strouse. © 1977 EDWIN H. MORRIS & COMPANY, A Division of MPL Communications, Inc. & CHARLES STROUSE. International Copyright Secured. All Rights Reserved. Used by permission.

10. Phillips Brooks, *Visions and Tasks* (New York: E.P. Dutton & Company, 1886), p. 330.

11. Henry van Dyke, *"Peace," The Poems of Henry van Dyke* (New York: Charles Scribner's Sons, 1939), p.12.